HOW TO GIVE

A Longer and Healthier Life

The complete owner's guide to caring for the older dog

CLAIRE BESSANT

PETER NEVILLE

BRADLEY VINER

Sg

SMITH GRYPHON PUBLISHERS

To old dogs and their owners everywhere

To my wife Liz, and children Emma and Oliver, who had to put up with my affair with a word processor, and to Elkie, my sweet Mutt who wandered into our lives 14 years ago and is presently re-teaching me almost everything I know about caring for elderly dogs – *Bradley*

To our daughter Sinead who, at 3, has shown us that there is no generation gap between species and to Muttley, aged 15, her pal. To the irrepressible Scud, who we confidently expect to barge into old age in the same way as he has barged through our lives so far – *Claire and Peter*

First published in Great Britain in 1994 by
SMITH GRYPHON LIMITED
Swallow House, 11–21 Northdown Street
London N1 9BN

Designed by Hammond Hammond

ISBN 1 85685 072 2

A CIP catalogue record for this book is available from the British Library

Phototypeset by Bessant Neville Partnership, Salisbury
Printed and bound by Hartnolls Ltd, Bodmin

CONTENTS

4
MEDICAL CARE

5
AILMENTS IN OLDER DOGS: AN A–Z

6
FOOD FOR HEALTH

7
BEHAVIOUR AT HOME

8
DOGS TOGETHER

9
OLD AGE COMFORTS

10
LETTING GO

INTRODUCTION

Some of the best things in life are those that have been with us for a long time – the big old armchair by the fire, the threadbare but comfortable slippers and the company of old friends. Old friends are the best because we have little to hide from them; they know our moods and our shortcomings and still accept us and love us. To many people one of their best friends is their older dog. Gone are those crazy puppy days: the disasters and disobedience have been replaced by companionship and a mutual admiration. As one lady in our survey on older dogs conducted in *Dogs Today* magazine commented, 'The best part of owning an old dog is that you get to know each other's reactions and view points and you have little routines . . . it is a sort of language that means you're not always having to call the dog and give commands. It's about sharing your home with the dog as a friend.'

However, it is just that warm and comfortable feeling which may lull you into a false sense of security about your dog. Because you see him every day you may not notice the changes which are occurring with age: his slowing up or increase in weight or stiffening of movements. How long our dogs live is affected not only by how we treat them in their latter years, but by how we manage and care for them throughout life. It is only when our dogs become ill and we sit down and look at them anew that we wonder why we have not noticed the little changes – the slowness, the dull coat or the fact that the dog is drinking a lot. Having a positive attitude and acting quickly could save your dog's life. Early treatment is much more likely to be successful. You are the greatest single factor determining how long the animal will live.

How to Give Your Dog a Longer and Healthier Life will help owners of dogs of all ages to keep an eye on their pets as the years go by. It explains what signs to look out for, how to keep the dog as fit as possible and how to make life comfortable for the older dog. As well as covering the physical and medical problems that may arise the book also explains some of the behaviour changes that can occur and how to cope with any problems they cause. It also gives advice on deciding on the right time for euthanasia, how to choose what you want to do with the body and how to cope with grief then move on and start again.

As we went through over 350 questionnaires from owners of older dogs, we were struck by the great feeling of love and devotion people had for their old friends, often despite great difficulties in keeping them going through illness or disability. We all want to feel we have done our best by our loyal companions and that we have given them a comfortable and happy life for as long as possible. What happens at the end is a culmination of all the previous years and it should go without saying that prevention is always better than cure. What you feed and how you care for and treat the puppy you have today may have a strong bearing on how well and fit it stays in years to come – those twilight years that can be the most rewarding of all for dog and owner alike.

1. Age and your dog

Our old dogs are very precious. Puppies are beautiful and playful, young dogs keen and handsome, but the old dog, even though perhaps slowing down a little, is worth his weight in gold. Gone are his days of chewing the furniture, teasing the postman and chasing the neighbour's cat (or perhaps still chasing, but no longer catching). Now he wears a wise and dignified look. Instead of the prankster, he has become the observer, usually to be found in front of the fire on his favourite chair. Of course, some breeds mature much later than others and certain dogs continue to act like pups all their lives, as many Labrador owners will tell you!

We see the changes in our new puppy, are amazed at its speed of growth and behaviour changes and notice when it has reached maturity (physical maturity anyway) at about a year old. However we often fail to recognise the third phase of our dog's life, that of old age, because the onset is gradual and by then the dog has slotted into our lives in a less intrusive way than the boisterous puppy. This has been described beautifully in a letter we received as part of a survey on old dogs. Brenda Kennedy wrote:

> *'Brynn, my oldie, has become dependable as he has matured, if he's quiet you know it's because he's asleep, not eating the house-plants! The best part of owning an old dog is that you get to know each other's reactions and viewpoints, you have little routines for meals, bedtimes and walks. It's a sort of language that means you're not always having to call the dog and give commands. It's about sharing your home with the dog as a friend, understanding each other's moods and respecting each other, knowing you can relax the rules a bit without being taken advantage of. As an older dog, Brynn has become so much more precious. His illnesses have*

required a lot of nursing, which has built up our relationship and trust in each other.'

Often we don't really notice how old our dogs are – we count for about six or seven years and thereafter say that the dog is about 8 until we have to take stock and actually work out how long we have had him. The counting problem is usually worse if we have a second dog which is referred to as 'the puppy' and is always 'young' because he is the younger of the two. It is not until the senior dog dies that we realise that young Ben is actually 10 years old!

HOW LONG DOES A DOG LIVE?

So how long does a dog live? A rough estimate would tell you that most dogs live between 8 and 15 years. However, unlike cats which are much of a uniform size and weight, dogs vary greatly from the mighty St Bernard or Mastiff (males regularly weigh up to 90 kg or 200 lb) to the tiny Chihuahua (weighing sometimes less than 1 kg (2 lb) and their average life expectancy shows equal range. For example, Irish Wolfhounds may only live to 7 to 8 years old, whereas small dogs such as Jack Russells commonly reach 15 and some even reach their twenties.

Dogs in their late teens are much less common than cats and they begin to show their age much earlier and much more dramatically. A survey carried out in the UK in 1986 found that about 10 per cent of dogs and cats in the country were between 8 and 10 years old, 7 per cent between 10 and 12 years old and 5 per cent between 12 and 14 years old. But only 2.5 per cent of dogs were over 14 as compared to 5 per cent of cats.

Cats also seem to have a shorter 'old' phase to their life than dogs. Perhaps they age more gracefully, and they certainly seem to avoid much of the stiffness which we associate with our old canine companions. While you might look at a 15-year-old cat and be unable to decide whether it is 5 or 15, there is no such leeway with dogs. Even the fittest and most long-lived breeds, such as Jack Russells and Border Collies, are probably greying and stiff by then. Of course there is great individual variability and it would be wrong to say all Great Danes had shorter lives than any other type of dog, but on average the giant breeds such as Great Danes, Irish Wolfhounds, Mastiffs and St Bernards rarely reach their teens and are often lucky to reach double figures.

Why different breeds have different life spans

Why should this be? Looking again at our feline pets we can see that there is very little variability between the size or weight of the breeds. Man has not really been able to change the form of the cat, except perhaps for body and head shape and length of coat. The efficient feline hunting machine which is exceptionally successful in the wild has remained remarkably unaltered. Even though there are many different breeds of cat they all seem to age at about the same rate. The Siamese is reputed to live the longest on average, perhaps because it is one of the slimmer breeds – a hint we may take note of in keeping our dogs from becoming overweight.

Now look at dogs. In the wild, the dog family does show some variation in size and shape, but Wild Dogs, Coyotes, Dingos and Wolves are all what we would call average sized, compared to the breeds we have engineered ourselves. If we let all our specialised breeds of dogs breed together we would return to the average-sized mutt – the dog of the best size and weight, agility and intelligence to survive scavenging and hunting for itself in the environment in which it lives. What we have done in creating our breeds is to choose those characteristics we want in our dogs, be it temperament, looks or working ability, and maintain them artificially by selective breeding. Along with the traits we want, we may have to put up with other inherited traits that may be harmful to the dog (see chapter 3), or that merely mean that its life span is unlikely to match that of the medium-sized mongrel with what we call 'hybrid vigour'.

However, some pedigree breeds are known for their longevity. From a survey we carried out with the readers of *Dogs Today* magazine, in which over 350 owners completed a questionnaire about their current old dogs and dogs they had previously owned, it was obvious that the Border Collie and the Jack Russell, along with the Whippet and other terriers were among the longest living. The Tibetan breeds are supposedly long lived too. One lady in our survey reported that her Jack Russell had died at the great age of 24 years.

It should not go unnoticed that these longer-lived breeds are highly active and not prone to putting on weight, one of the factors which will be considered in chapter 3. They also have long noses and so do not suffer from breathing problems like some of the branchycephalic (short nosed) breeds such as Pugs, Bulldogs, Boxers etc. Some of the findings on expected average lifespan of breeds from our survey are listed in the table on page 6. However, none get anywhere near matching the dogs listed in the *Guinness Book of Records*. The greatest reliable age recorded for a dog is 29 years and 5 months for an Australian Cattle Dog named Bluey who came from Victoria in Australia. The dog was obtained as a puppy in 1910 and worked among cattle and sheep for nearly 20 years before being put to sleep on November 14, 1939. In the UK, a Welsh Collie named Taffy from Bromwich in the West Midlands lived for 27 years and 313 days before he died in 1980. The oldest cat on record lived to 36 – it is very doubtful whether this will ever be matched by the canine species.

Of course not everyone owns a pedigree dog and the cross-breeds or mongrels are often well ahead on the longevity stakes, probably because they are becoming more like that average-sized, average-weight mutt discussed earlier. If that cross-breed is made up partly of Jack Russell, Border Collie or one of the longer-lived breeds then it also seems to have great longevity. In our own survey, the cross breed or mongrel had an average age of just over 12 years with a range of ages from 3 to 17 years old. Of the 69 dogs aged 14 years and over, 19 were Collie or Collie cross, 13 Jack Russell or Jack Russell cross, 5 Golden Retriever, 7 Labrador or Labrador cross and the rest were all different breeds. The oldest dogs were age 17, 18 and 24; a Poodle, Jack Russell, 3 Collie crosses and a Terrier cross. However, it is important to look not only at the average but at the range of ages covered by the statistics. As you can see from the table below 17 years is not an uncommon age for some of the longer lived individuals within a breed and again the same breeds appear – the Jack Russell, Poodle, Border Collie, Yorkshire Terrier.

Dog breeds and their ages

Dog breed	Number	Av. age (yrs)	Range (yrs)
Jack Russell	9	14.3	10 - 24
Yorkshire Terrier	5	13.8	10 - 17
Shih Tzu	8	13.8	11 - 15
Labrador	33	12.7	5 - 17
Springer Spaniel	9	12.6	10 - 16
Dachshund	16	12.5	9 - 17
Staffordshire Terrier	6	12.5	7 - 17
Mongrel/cross	97	12.4	3 -17
Cairn Terrier	11	12.4	11 - 16
Poodle	12	12.2	4 - 18

Border Collie	22	12.0	2 - 20
Golden Retriever	18	11.8	8 - 15
Corgi	18	11.7	9 - 14
Sheltie	8	11.7	10 - 14
Boxer	14	11.2	6 - 14
Chihuahua	6	11.5	9 - 15
Pekingese	8	10.7	6 - 15
GSD	32	9.5	2 - 14

KEEPING THE PUPPY IN YOUR DOG

The world over, people are looking for the secret of youth or at least for ways to hold back the ageing process. While there may be no miraculous answer, we sometimes fail to recognise the huge changes in life expectancy that have come about only fairly recently. Improving medical care and knowledge of diet and lifestyle gives us all the option to live longer than our counterparts even 50 years ago. The same is true for our dogs. Veterinary care has come on in leaps and bounds from a time only a few decades ago when the pet dog was hardly recognised, and when working breeds were cared for only until their usefulness was over, often treated in a merely functional manner along with other farm animals.

Attitudes towards pets have changed and the dog or cat is now viewed as a member of the family. The pet food and care industry is huge and innovations in diet and treatment mean that like us our dogs are living longer and surviving illnesses or diseases which would have killed them in years gone past. Indeed, some veterinary care is ahead of medical treatment because the research has been carried out on animals and has yet to be used for people. These factors, along with others which affect how long a dog can live, are tackled in chapter 3.

How to calculate your dog's age

The standard way of comparing a cat or dog's age with that of a human being is to multiply its age by seven. Thus a 1-year-old would be 7, a 2-year-old 14, a 12 year old 84 and a 20-year-old 140 and so on. However, this does not really equate very well with the life stages of the dog and we now have a much better comparative method which makes a great deal more sense.

Here's how to calculate your dog's age in human terms. The first year of the dog's life can be taken as an equivalent to 15 human years. By the time it is 2, the dog can be considered the equivalent of a 24-year-old person. Thereafter each year can be taken as four human years. Thus a 12-year-old is 64 (24 + 10x4).

When you start to look at a dog's life, all of this makes a great deal more sense. For example, in its first year the dog becomes weaned, learns to be independent of its mother, to live with a new family and it is usually sexually mature by a year old. Most humans, too, are physically able to reproduce by the age of 15. A 2-year-old dog is quite an experienced creature and has just about fathomed out routines and what it wants from those around it, as well as how to control them. Dogs usually settle down by the time they are 4 years old – the equivalent of about 32 human years.

Although most cats can be considered middle-aged at about 8 years old, with canines there is a wider range simply because of breed differences. An 8-year-old Great Dane would be considered old, whereas a Border Collie of the same age may still be running 70 miles a day herding the sheep over the hills or winning agility competitions. It is probably best to look at groupings of dogs – the giants such as Great Danes, Irish Wolfhounds, Mastiffs, and St Bernards being the shortest lived; the middle range are those such as Labradors, Golden Retrievers, Setters; the third group of smaller dogs, or those which are very active like Collies, seem to have the greatest life expectancy. For group one the transition from middle age to old age could be as early as 4 or 5 years old; for group two it would be about 6 or 7, and the third group may not be leaving middle age until about 8 or 9 years old.

These ages give a rough indication as to when we should be starting to notice changes in our pets and to check them over regularly. It doesn't matter if you start monitoring your dog too early – it's better to catch problems sooner rather than later. For more on this, see chapter 4.

What is your dog's real age?

Look up your dog's age is on the left side of the bone and and see how old he really is by reading across to the human years.

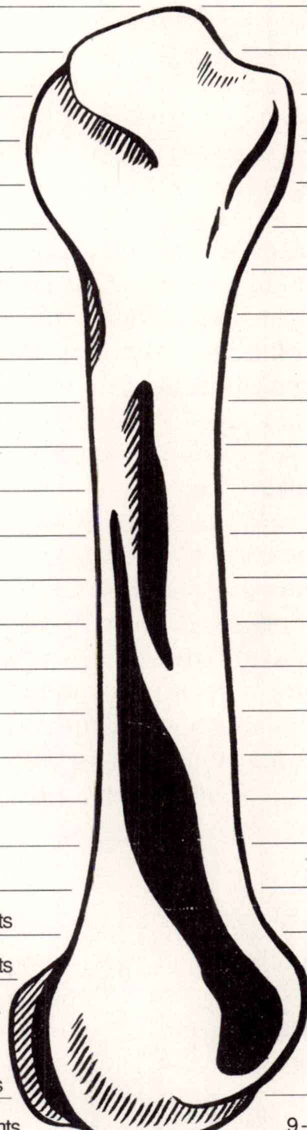

DOGS	YEARS	YEARS	HUMANS
	22	104	AMAZING
VERY RARE TO PASS 20	21	100	
	20	96	OLD
	19	92	
EXCEPTIONAL DOGS	18	88	
	17	84	
	16	80	
	15	76	
SMALLER ACTIVE BREEDS STILL GOING STRONG	14	72	ACTIVE BUT AGING
	13	68	
AVERAGE LIFE SPAN FOR DOGS	12	64	
	11	60	RETIREMENT
	10	56	
	9	52	MENOPAUSE
MIDDLE AGE	8	48	MIDDLEAGE SPREAD
	7	44	
SLOWING DOWN FOR GIANT BREEDS	6	40	
	5	36	
	4	32	CAREER MAKING
	3	28	
	2	24	MATURITY
	14 mts	18	ADULT
PHYSICAL MATURITY	12 mts	15	
	6mts	12	SEXUAL MATURITY
ADULT COMMUNICATION	4 mts	2-3	TALKING
DOG WEANED	2-3 mts	9-12 mts	BABY WEANED

2. Signs of ageing

Dogs, just like people, exhibit great variations in how they age and how much they show that age. Some look positively ancient when they are 3 years old (human equivalent 28 years old), while others never have a grey hair in their lives. However, looking old may not mean the same as feeling old or ill. Indeed we need to understand that old age does not equate to illness. Ageing is a normal and predictable process of life. Granted the scales are tipped towards degeneration rather than regeneration and growth but this does not necessarily mean that any illness which occurs cannot be treated.

'Old age' is not a disease. It is just that illness is more common when we are older and often several diseases or upsets may occur together rather than one at a time as they did earlier in life. Many older pets may have mild to moderate degrees of several diseases at the same time – this is the challenge facing veterinary surgeons treating the animal. Each problem needs to be diagnosed individually as well as being treated in combination with others, taking into consideration the impact of each disease on the body systems.

AGE-RELATED CHANGES

Some age-related changes such as vision and hearing loss cannot be prevented. Other examples are loss of flexibility and loss of muscle and nerve cells. In general there is a gradual reduction in the animal's capabilities from the age of 5 to 7 years (depending mostly on the size of the dog). One of the most important things to remember about older pets (and people for that matter) is that they have a decreasing ability to survive stress, be it illness, rehoming, diet alterations or merely a change in routine.

However the onset of clinical signs of many diseases can be delayed or successfully treated when caught early or when other health risks are reduced. The challenge to dog owners and veterinarians alike is to manage the impact of the body changes in such a way to keep the dog as healthy and active for as long as possible. A negative attitude will be self-fulfilling – not tackling a problem early may mean you leave it too late to treat it effectively. If we can understand some of the changes going on within our own or our dog's body we may be able to understand some of its limitations as well as having a positive attitude towards tackling problems which occur. Think about the 10-year-old dog – this is equivalent to a 56-year-old person – would you like to be written off at 56?

SKIN AND COAT CHANGES One of the first things we may notice about our dogs as they age is greying of the hair around the muzzle or eyes. Later the paws may also go grey and the coat become dull or thin. Of course just how noticeable this is depends on the breed and colour of the dog. Some do seem to go grey at a fairly early age – if the dog has a dark mask or muzzle, such as a boxer, whitening of the black hairs is easily seen. Obviously greying is much less noticeable on white dogs!

The skin is affected by hormonal changes in old age and by the fact that not so much oxygen is getting to all the hair follicles. Indeed where there were five hairs per follicle in youth, in old age there may be only two or three, hence the coat becomes more sparse. The skin also thickens and becomes less pliable, while the very outside layer (the epidermis) may become in itself very thin. The loss of that youthful lustre is often a very slow process and one we may not notice unless we take a long hard look at our dogs from time to time.

Larger dogs may form callouses at pressure points such as elbows. The skin may become drier or greasier than previously, depending on how the sebaceous glands are acting – in some dogs they can become more active, in others less so. These changes are not life-threatening, but merely signs that the dog's body is not repairing itself quite so well as it did in its youth. Some changes may predispose the dog to skin cancers and a vigilant owner will notice any lumps or bumps and have them checked out at their veterinary surgery. Some may be simple harmless warts or lumps, but they are always worth checking. Generally the skin repairs itself less rapidly and as the immune system is less efficient there is more risk of infection.

THE DIGESTIVE SYSTEM The digestive system (the mouth, teeth, tongue, oesophagus, stomach and intestinal tract) processes foods, absorbs nutrients and turns the solid waste into faeces to be removed from the body. We all know how ill we can feel if our digestive system is not functioning well, even if it is just an upset stomach. We must also remember that the teeth and their ability to prepare food for digestion are vital to the wellbeing of the digestive system. An infection in the mouth can result in infections elsewhere or an illness caused by the toxins producted by the infection. Age also decreases the sense of taste as the number of taste buds decline.

Olfaction or the sense of smell is usually the first sensory system to show the effect of age. Less saliva may be produced and the acid produced by the stomach may diminish, which can result in vomiting, flatulence and sometimes diarrhoea. As the body ages it does not produce digestive enzymes quite so effectively and so digestion may be slowed or some nutrients absorbed less effectively than before. The cells lining the digestive system are constantly being replaced, but this can slow in old age, again affecting the digestion. When we realise that these changes are occurring we can see why dramatic changes in an old dog's diet can be very harmful, and why a raid on the dustbin which produced nothing more than a burp in puppyhood now produces a full scale digestive upset! See chapters 5 and 6 for a more detailed outline of tackling digestive problems.

THE CARDIOVASCULAR SYSTEM The heart and all the blood vessels associated with it are also affected by the ageing process. In the last third of the dog's life the output from its heart decreases by one third. Add to this the fact that the veins and arteries have become thickened and so are narrower, making it harder to pump blood around the body to provide oxygen and remove waste, and you realise why the old mutt sometimes seems a little more puffed out than usual. Heart disease does occur in dogs and one group of investigators estimated that in dogs between 9 and 12 there was an incidence of 25 per cent; in dogs 13 years and older this rises to 33 per cent. Because the bone marrow is less effective in the renewal of red blood cells which carry oxygen to all parts of the body, this may take twice as long as when the dog was a puppy. The animal's immune system will also be less efficient as white blood cells may not be so active or plentiful.

THE RESPIRATORY SYSTEM In old age the respiratory system becomes less elastic and the capacity of the lungs is reduced. These various changes mean that oxygen may not get to all body cells as effectively as it used to. Animals may also be more prone to inflammation or infection of the respiratory tract.

THE URINARY SYSTEM The urinary system removes waste from the body in the form of urine. As animals get older the system becomes less efficient not only in reabsorbing water (and thus more urine is produced) but also at removing all the waste products from the blood. These toxins can build up in the body causing illness.

MUSCLES AND BONES In old age, muscles and bones become less dense; muscles lose some of their elasticity and bones can become brittle. Excessive exercise can cause inflammation and pain. Often joints are affected by arthritis and the joint surfaces may degerate further causing a very painful condition.

THE NERVOUS SYSTEM Older dogs react less quickly to things around them – it is said that when a dog is in its prime, messages are transmitted up and down the nerves at approximately 225 miles per hour. This slows to about 50 miles per hour in older pets. Signs of senility can be the same in dogs as in man. Some affected dogs can become irritable when disturbed, slow to respond and have problems with orientation. One of the first signs may be loss of house training.

SIGHT, HEARING AND TASTE Increased age can bring profound changes to the senses of smell, hearing and sight. These changes may be so gradual that owners do not notice them and the dog itself learns to cope with them, or they may be very sudden. In the eyes cataract formations are common, along with other changes which make vision less clear. You may notice the eyes change colour at about 8 or 9 years old. They may look a little cloudy or white or blue. Hearing loss is common from about 10 years old and there may also be increased risk of ear infection. See also chapters 4, 6 and 9.

AGEING AND YOUR DOG

Below are some of the findings of our survey of over 350 dogs. These are the changes that their owners noticed, and the ages at which they began to occur.

GOING GREY We asked owners if their dogs showed signs of ageing. Of owners of 8-year-olds 36 per cent said no, as did 20 per cent of owners of 9 and 10-year-olds; 14 per cent of 11-year-olds and 11 per cent of 12-year-olds. Only 6 per cent owning 13 and 14-year-olds and none owning 15 or 16-year-olds and above said their dogs showed no signs of ageing. The most common first noted sign of old age was greying or whitening of the hair on the muzzle and around the eyes. Some owners reported that the colours of their black/brown/white animals changed and the dark spots became lighter, if not white. Different breeds and colours of dogs may show changes earlier – many breeds get grey chins fairly early on but, on average greying seems to begin at about 6 to 7 years old.

STIFFNESS The other most commonly reported sign of ageing was a stiffening of legs or back either on a walk or after returning home. About one third of owners mentioned arthritis or stiffness in 8-9-year-olds; in 10-11-year-olds this rose to 45 per cent; in 12-13-year-olds 62 per cent mentioned it and almost 70 per cent of owners of 14-year-olds mentioned that their pets became stiff. Stiffness or seemingly painful movement got worse in cold or wet weather, or in the morning, and many dogs were reluctant to go out in very inclement weather. Other dogs had wobbly or shaky hindquarters which caused problems during or after exercise. Most people said their dogs were much more tired after exercise and often lagged at the end of a walk or going uphill; others sat down when tired; others wheezed or coughed. Many panted in warm weather and needed help into the car or up the stairs.

HEARING Hearing did not seem to be a problem in most dogs until about 10 years old and only then about 10 per cent of owners of 10 and 11-year-olds mentioned it. However, this rose to 27 per cent of 12-year-olds and 45 per cent of 13 and 14-year-olds. From 15 years onwards, over 60 per cent of owners mentioned hearing problems.

SIGHT Cloudy, blueing, or milky white colour changes in eyes, and cataract formation, are also obvious signs of ageing and again owners did not mention them until their dogs were about 10 years old. About 30 per cent of 12 and 13-year-olds had sight problems and this rose sharply to 52 per cent at 13 years, 60 per cent in 15-year-olds and 75 per cent in dogs older than this. Several owners mentioned that their pet's eyes were more watery or runny.

SLEEP Most owners mentioned that their dogs slept more as they aged. By 11 years old more than 80 per cent said their dog slept more and this increased to over 90 per cent by 15 years. Sleep patterns changed and dogs often took themselves off to bed more frequently or collapsed to sleep after exercise. Chapters 7 and 9 deal with the ways of accommodating different sleep patterns and position, and of making older dogs more relaxed, secure and comfortable and reassuring them if they feel vulnerable.

EXERCISE Of all respondents for all ages of dog, only 19 said their pet did not enjoy exercise at all. Some said that they did not seem to enjoy it as much as in their youth – this figure ranged from 20 per cent of 8-year-olds to 60 per cent of the 16-year-olds. We asked if dogs only 'pottered about in the garden' – surprisingly only 42 (12 per cent) of owners said their dog did this instead of going out for a walk, even at a very old age. Most dogs still asked to go out – almost 80 per cent of the 15-year-olds still asked to go for a walk.

Over half of the 8 and 9-year-olds walked two to four miles a day and this decreased slowly to 7 per cent of 15-year-olds. Even at 14 years old over 40 per cent of dogs walked over one mile a day. However at 15 years and over, half a percent were exercised for under half a mile each day, and most of the rest for under a mile.

Up to the age of 11 more than half of the owners said their dogs did not suffer problems when out on walks – at 12 this fell to 50 per cent and thereafter the number with problems such as stiffness or weak legs, breathing problems, slowing or lagging increased to 85 per cent at 15 and 16 years old. The same is true for dogs suffering after-affects of a walk, these being stiffness, extreme tiredness or wobbly legs/back end. So it seems that the spirit is still willing to walk but sometimes the older flesh is a bit weak!

CHARACTER CHANGES Most dogs mellow with age; others get grumpy – this is covered in detail in chapters 7 and 8.

3. Fit for life

There are more than 400 breeds of domesticated dog in the world today, and they vary enormously in size and shape. There is no doubt that breeding can play a major part in the life expectancy of a particular dog.

The size factor

The first factor is simply that of size – as discussed in chapter 1, generally the larger the dog, the shorter its average lifespan. Toy breeds such as Yorkshire Terriers commonly live to be 15 or 16, whereas at the other extreme, giant breeds such as the St Bernard can be considered pretty elderly by the time they are 8, and only rarely survive past 10 years of age. The oldest dog in our *Dogs Today* survey was a Jack Russell Terrier that had reached the grand old age of 24! It's not fully understood why there should be this relationship between size and decreasing life expectancy, although it would seem logical that when the size of the dog is stretched to its limits, greater strain is put upon organs such as its heart and lungs. As we shall see later, heart disease is a common killer in the giant breeds.

Pedigree or mongrel?

Mongrel or cross-breed dogs tend to have a longer life expectancy than a pedigree dog of a similar size. This is not in itself due to 'bad breeding', but because of what is known as hybrid vigour as outlined in chapter 1. We all carry two genes for each particular characteristic that is passed on genetically, one gene from each parent. Many hereditary faults are caused by recessive traits – that is, both genes have to be carrying the abnormal trait for it to cause an abnormality to develop. The more closely related the parents, the greater the chance that each will carry the harmful recessive gene for a particular condition. This leads to a greater incidence of hereditary diseases in pedigree dogs, who also seem to be that little bit less hardy than your average mutt. Of course, it is the breeding of related dogs together that has produced the variety of breeds that we enjoy today. Although careful selection of breeding stock can help to eliminate dogs that are known to be carrying hereditary diseases from the further breeding, it will never be possible to eliminate hereditary diseases entirely.

Inherited problems

There are a wide range of inherited diseases that can be found in one breed or another. Some of them are so severe that the puppy dies before birth or when it is very young. Fortunately, most of them are very rare and do not need to trouble us. The three main groups of inherited diseases that may affect the health of the dog in later years are those that affect the joints, hereditary eye diseases, and, in some cases, congenital heart disease. The latter can sometimes be hereditary (that is, passed from one generation to another), or may be developmental (simply a fault in the growth of an embryo that is a one-off occurrence). Severe congenital heart problems will cause problems early in life, but it is possible for a mild disorder to remain undetected until later years (*see* Heart Disease pp.50).

HIP DYSPLASIA The most common hereditary disorder to affect the joints is hip dysplasia – a tendency for the hips to dislocate out of their sockets, causing arthritis to develop in the joint. This is common in most of the large breeds of dog, and in severe cases will cause lameness at around six to nine months, but milder cases may not show obvious signs of the problem until arthritis sets in later on in life. Osteochondritis dissecans is another hereditary disorder that affects the joints of dogs. This causes an ulcer to develop in the cartilage that lines the joint, which then leads on to arthritis. This seems to be becoming more common, and particularly affects the elbow joints of larger breeds of dog, although it can also occur in the stifle (knee) and hock (ankle). Smaller breeds can also be affected by inherited joint diseases – luxating patella is a condition where the kneecap has a tendency to slip out of the groove in the femur (thigh bone) along which it normally slides. This affects toy breeds such as Yorkshire Terriers and Chihuahuas, and avascular necrosis of the femoral head can cause hip problems in small terriers. All of these problems are primarily diseases that can cause trouble in young dogs and may lead to chronic arthritis in later life.

EYE DISEASE There are a wide range of hereditary eye diseases that can cause loss of vision. Although dogs are born with the condition, some types of hereditary eye disease do not show until the dog reaches middle age, and can result in blindness in the older dog. (*see* Blindness, pp.41). The most common inherited eye diseases are progressive retinal atrophy, which causes a gradual deterioration in the retina at the back of the eye, and hereditary cataracts, which cause a cloudiness of the lens to develop.

Check before you buy

When you first purchase a pedigree puppy, it's advisable to familiarise yourself with the hereditary problems that commonly occur in that breed. Question the breeder to make sure he or she has been taking all reasonable steps to breed only from bloodlines that are known to be free of disease. In particular, health schemes exist to help reduce the incidence of hip dysplasia and some of the hereditary eye diseases.

It may seem strange to talk about purchasing a puppy in a book about elderly dogs, but the right start can have an important effect on the dog's health later on. Don't hesitate to contact your veterinary surgeon for advice even before you choose your new puppy.

BEHAVIOURAL PROBLEMS

One of the most alarming facts in our pet-loving western world is that, every year, millions of young dogs are destroyed by veterinarians and animal welfare societies around the world. Not all of them die because there aren't enough homes for all the dogs that are born, and not all of them are killed because of incurable disease or to relieve suffering occurring as a result of some terrible injury. They are killed at the request of their owners because some aspect of their behaviour is so unacceptable that the only answer to the problem seems to be to destroy the dog. The numbers killed outnumber the incidence of dying from other causes - the condition, 'behaviour problem', could be considered to have reached epidemic proportions.

Most of the dogs which are killed because they have a behaviour problem, could have been treated successfully by one of the growing number of pet behaviour therapists and many could have been prevented if owners had been offered the right advice about choosing, acquiring, looking after and relating to their pet.

Coping with adolescence

This depressing picture emphasises that one of the key factors influencing whether any domestic dog will live to enjoy its old age is how it behaves as a young dog and how well its owners bond with it and react to any problems. Caring for a puppy is usually fun and owners will forgive a lot. Mishaps and unacceptable antics usually encourage the teaching of more acceptable behaviour, but our tolerance levels start to diminish rapidly once the puppy starts to become a dog. Sometimes, quite wrongly, we start to ascribe malice, social scheming, plotting and forethought to the adolescent dog. The development of secondary sexual characteristics in response to the production of various hormones at this stage of life causes increasing social awareness, and sometimes competitiveness, in the young dog as it attempts to find its place in its human family and to learn how to relate to other dogs both at home and outside.

It is during adolescence that aggression problems towards owners, visitors and other dogs usually first appear. At the same time it becomes difficult for the owner to control a now larger and stronger pet. Equally, a young dog may become over-attached to one or more members of its family and be psychologically unable to cope without their physical company. This can lead to displacement behaviours such as chewing and destruction of household furnishings and manic repetitive barking and howling when the dog has to be left at home alone.

Help is at hand

Adolescence is an extremely difficult period for dog and owner alike, but the same is true for virtually any social mammal, as any parent of an adolescent child could doubtless testify! So it's no surprise, given the difficulties that families encounter with their own adolescent children, that we should have such a high failure rate with dogs of this age. The crucial difference is, of course, that we generally don't rehome or euthanase our kids, however tempting it may be on occasions. For the harassed owner, there is now a great deal of information and help available on canine behaviour. Many veterinary surgeons or dog clubs hold puppy classes where puppies can learn to interact with each other and people and owners can learn how to handle potential problems and what to look out for – more of this in chapter 7. If you are experiencing behaviour problems your vet may refer you to one of the members of the Association of Pet Behaviour Counsellors (257 Royal College Street, London NW1 9LY). The APBC also has a list of puppy classes which are being run around the country.

Fortunately, providing a dog survives its adolescence and integrates well into its human pack as an adult, advances in diet and veterinary care mean that the outlook for a long and natural life-span is probably better now than ever before. Behaviour changes are likely to occur as the dog enters old age and certain behaviour problems may arise but, after a lifetime of good relations, owners will usually be as tolerant and understanding as they were when the dog was a puppy.

MEDICAL PROBLEMS

Medical problems may affect the dog's chances of living out his natural lifespan at any stage of life.

Vaccination is vital

There is a very high awareness of the need to vaccinate puppies against several important infectious diseases, but too many owners allow the annual booster vaccinations to lapse. Whilst it is true that these serious infections are most common among the young, they can strike at any age. An annual vaccination not only helps to maintain protection, but also provides a vital opportunity for your vet to give your dog an annual health check and for you to discuss any problems concerning your pet that may be worrying you. At the present time, we are able to vaccinate against the following diseases in the UK.

DISTEMPER One of the major killers of dogs before a vaccine was developed, this highly infectious disease is caused by a virus that initially causes signs of coughing, running eyes and nose, and diarrhoea. If a dog survives this initial phase of the disease, the virus can then go on to affect the brain, causing fits. Once a dog reaches this stage, euthanasia is the only kind option. Although the disease is most common in young dogs, it can sometimes affect elderly dogs. Dogs that have been infected with the virus as puppies and recover, sometimes develop a disorder of the dental enamel known as 'distemper teeth' that can cause dental problems later in life.

HEPATITIS Infectious canine hepatitis is a viral infection that affects the lining of the blood vessels, particularly in the liver. It causes acute vomiting, diarrhoea and internal bleeding and is often rapidly fatal. It only affects younger animals.

LEPTOSPIROSIS This disease is caused by a bacterium rather than a virus, and the dog is commonly affected by one of two species, one that primarily affects the liver and one that attacks the kidneys. Infection can occur from the urine of other dogs or from rodent's urine, and can be passed on to humans. A bout of leptospirosis contracted early in life can scar the kidneys and cause kidney failure to develop in later life.

PARVOVIRUS This is a relatively new disease of dogs, that first caused serious epidemics in the later 1970s and killed many dogs before an effective vaccine was developed. It causes severe gastroenteritis, and although it is most severe in young dogs, it can affect dogs of any age.

PARAINFLUENZA Not nearly as serious as the diseases outlined above, this virus is one of the causes of kennel cough, an infectious cough that can be quite troublesome, especially to an old dog, but not usually life-threatening.

BORDETELLA BRONCHISEPTICA This is the most important cause of kennel cough, and is a bacterium quite closely related to the one that causes whooping cough in children. Vaccination is not given by injection, but as drops administered into the nose – much to the bewilderment of many canine patients! This vaccine is advisable for any dogs that are being exposed to a high risk of the disease, such as before entering boarding kennels, and is particularly important in elderly dogs that might be more seriously affected by this infection.

RABIES The UK is thankfully free of rabies, and strict quarantine regulations keep it at bay. Because of this, rabies vaccination is not permitted in this country, except for dogs that are being exported overseas. Six months in quarantine is an awfully long time for a dog in its later years, and for this reason owners should avoid importing an elderly dog into this country if at all possible.

FOOD FACTS

Just as we are becoming aware that a healthy diet throughout our lives can help us to live to a ripe old age, we now realise that although it may be possible to rear a dog on a diet that is far from ideal, feeding the best balance of nutrients early on in life can have a marked effect upon health in later years. We will deal with diets specifically for elderly dogs in chapter 6.

Wet or dry?

We spend over £600 million pounds each year in the UK on prepared dog foods, and the major manufacturers put a great deal of effort into ensuring that the foods that we buy are balanced and safe. About three-quarters of the market is in canned dog foods, known as 'moist' because they have a high water content, but the demand for complete, dry dog foods is growing rapidly each year, and in many other countries the market is dominated by these dry foods. It does not matter if you feed a moist, semi-moist or dry dog food, since the dog will simply drink extra to make up the difference, providing you always have a supply of fresh drinking water available. It is, however, important to be aware of whether the food you are feeding is a complete food that contains everything the dog needs, or if it is designed to be fed with a mixer. Most dry foods fall into the former category and most canned foods into the latter, but feeding directions on the label should always be read carefully when a new food is purchased. Many owners make the mistake of using a completely dry food as if it were a mixer, and adding canned food or fresh meat to it. This unbalances a food that has been carefully prepared to ensure that all the nutrients are present in the correct balance, and can cause long-term problems.

Is fresh food better?

Many owners feel that simply doling out food from a packet or a can cannot be as good as lovingly preparing a special diet for their dog. They also feel that dogs get bored with the same old food day after day. Whilst it is perfectly possible to provide an adequate diet from fresh foods, it requires far more care and attention to make sure that all the levels of protein, carbohydrate, fat, fibre, vitamins and minerals are correct. Feeding household scraps makes it even more difficult to regulate the food intake, and the digestive system of many dogs is often simply unable to cope with the wide variety of rich foods that we humans eat. Once dogs are trained to receive their own food in their own bowl at a regular feeding time, they seem to be remarkably satisfied in being given the identical food day after day. Feeding scraps can lead to a faddy appetite and the dog may eventually train its owner to feed a diet that may be very tasty but is extremely unbalanced, such as pure meat.

Different foods for differing needs . . .

We are becoming increasingly aware that the nutritional requirements of the dog will vary depending upon the stage in its life and level of activity, and a range of foods designed to meet these varying needs is now available. In particular, puppies should be fed a food that provides the higher level of protein, energy, minerals and vitamins that puppies require. Working dogs may also need a special high-energy diet, and pregnant and lactating bitches certainly have particular feeding needs.

Fit not fat

Most dogs are natural gluttons, and far and away the most common problem resulting from bad feeding is obesity, which affects approximately one third of all pet dogs in the United Kingdom. There is no doubt that being seriously overweight will have a marked effect upon the health of the dog in later life, as it increases the incidence of many important diseases such as arthritis, diabetes, heart disease, chronic bronchitis and certain types of tumours.

Prevention is always better than cure, and you should weigh your dog regularly to see if the weight is gradually creeping up. Cutting down on starchy foods such as biscuits may be enough to control the problem, and you can satiate the appetite by feeding high fibre foodstuffs such as wheat bran or boiled cabbage. If this is not doing the trick, you should ask your vet to recommend a special low calorie food to help reduce weight, and a complete change of diet on to one of these foods is always very effective if adhered to strictly. Many owners are concerned when their pampered pooch refuses to eat the new diet, but dogs are very resistant to any harmful side-effects from starvation, and once the dog realises that nothing else is forthcoming they invariably do start to eat. Many veterinary surgeries run obesity clinics with regular weighing and advice sessions to help owners to get their pets to lose weight.

TAKING CARE OF THE TEETH

Dental disease is extremely common in middle-aged and older dogs. One advantage of dry dog foods is that they help to exercise the teeth and slow down the accumulation of tartar and scale which eventually causes gum disease and tooth loss. Hide chews will also help to prevent this build-up and are better than bones, which can crack the teeth and also cause digestive problems if swallowed. But regular toothbrushing is the most effective means of all, keeping the teeth in tip-top condition.

It should be started from puppyhood so that the dog gets used to regular toothbrushing as part of the grooming routine. Although the puppy teeth will fall out and be replaced by the permanent teeth, establishing the habit will reap dividends once the dog gets older. If you haven't started brushing early in life, it's never too late to start. Acclimatise your dog gradually, initially by gently rubbing the gums with your finger covered with a piece of gauze, then using dog toothpaste on the gauze and finally using a soft toothbrush.

KEEPING PARASITES AT BAY

It's most unlikely that a heavy burden of internal parasites, such as worms, or external parasites, such as fleas, early in life will have a long-term effect upon the health of your pet, but they are very common. Preventative health care against parasites should be carried out throughout your dog's life.

WORMS Roundworm and tapeworm are the most common intestinal parasites and the most effective wormers are available 'over the counter' from your veterinary surgery. Even if worms are unlikely to severely affect the health of your elderly dog, there is a slight health risk to humans from roundworm larvae, so you should worm your dog at least every six months even if you don't see any sign of worms.

FLEAS There are an increasing number of new products available in the fight against external parasites such as fleas, and since fleas lay their eggs around the home, it is certainly best to prevent them from getting a chance to establish themselves. Obviously, insecticides must be used to kill adult insects on the dog, but hormones that disrupt the life cycle of the flea can now be given in tablet form to all cats and dogs in the household – rather like putting the fleas onto a contraceptive pill! This type of drug is completely harmless to mammals and is probably the ideal long-term method of control.

SEX AND YOUR DOG

There's more to neutering your dog than simply birth control, and spaying a bitch or castrating a male dog can have a marked effect upon their health in later life.

The benefits of spaying

Bitches have a season twice a year, and it is generally accepted that having repeated litters is not good for their long-term health, or for the unwanted dog population. Your bitch's wild ancestors would have had a litter every season, but a large proportion of the puppies would die, and her life expectancy would be much shorter than a pet dog. It is, of course, possible to keep a bitch from having puppies by keeping her strictly confined during her season, but apart from avoiding the regular inconvenience of seasons, there are several important advantages in having her spayed (an operation to remove the womb and ovaries):

- The risk of an accidental mis-mating is removed.
- The incidence of mammary cancer is reduced – a very common problem in older, unspayed bitches.
- Womb infections cannot occur – again, very common in the elderly bitch and necessitating an emergency hysterectomy.
- The risk of cancer of the ovaries and womb is removed.

Any side effects are relatively minor. Although spaying is a major abdominal operation, the risks with modern anaesthetics and surgical techniques are very slight indeed, and many vets are carrying out the operation before the first season, when the womb is tiny and the risk of post-operative bleeding is lowest. Hair growth can be affected, and some breeds such as Setters can develop rather a woolly coat, but this is purely cosmetic. Potentially more serious is the incidence of urinary incontinence after the operation – a leaking of urine when the bitch lies down, but in most cases this can be controlled by giving a regular supplement of female hormones in tablet form.

The final side-effect is a tendency of the bitch to use her food more efficiently after neutering, which means that she may be more prone to put on weight if fed the same amount of food. This can easily be avoided by monitoring her weight regularly and slightly decreasing the food intake if necessary, or switching to one of the 'light' dog foods with a mildly reduced calorie content, designed not to take weight off your pet but to prevent her from putting it on.

The decision to put a healthy bitch through an operation that may not seem strictly necessary may be a difficult one, but vets that have to cope with the very serious yet avoidable problems of breast cancer and womb infections later in life do not usually hesitate to recommend the operation.

To castrate or not?

The beneficial effects upon health in old age are not as clear cut in the male dog as in the female and the problems of regular seasons do not arise, but there are still several health advantages to be gained by castrating a dog when he is young:

- Prostatic disorders are prevented.
- Tumours of the testicles cannot occur.
- Peri-anal adenomas – a growth that quite commonly develops around the anus of elderly dogs – are less likely to develop.

If anything, the operation is less major than spaying a bitch because the testicles are external to the body. It is worth mentioning retained testicles, where one or both testicles fail to descend from the abdominal cavity down into the scrotum in early puppyhood. These testicles should definitely be removed whilst the dog is young (perhaps at around a year of age), as they are not maintained at the slightly lower than body temperature in the scrotum and therefore are much more likely to develop into a tumour as the dog gets older.

Castrated male dogs may, like bitches, develop woolly coats, and weight gain can also be a problem unless preventative steps are taken. Most vets do not recommend routine castration of male dogs unless they suffer from a particular behavioural problem that is likely to be helped by neutering, such as aggression with other male dogs, urine marking around the house, or a strong desire to roam. If castration is being considered for one of these reasons, it is worth remembering that the operation can have several beneficial health effects later on in life.

Insure for peace of mind

A sudden accident or illness can present an owner with an unexpected bill for veterinary care. There is much that can be done with modern veterinary treatment, even with the most severe problem, but a course of treatment could run to several hundred pounds. Many dog owners are not aware that for around £2 a week they can take out pet insurance to cover veterinary costs – the owner only has to pay an initial excess of of around £30 for any particular course of treatment, and the rest can be claimed back from the insurance company up to the policy limit, usually around £1000. Of course, preventative care such as vaccinations is not covered, but there are often other useful benefits included, such as third party cover, payment for advertising and offering a reward for a lost dog, holiday cancellation costs if your dog needs emergency surgery before you go away on holiday, and boarding kennel fees if you have to go into hospital.

Most companies will only insure a dog if it is under 10 years of age when the policy is initially taken out, but then they will undertake to continue that cover for the rest of its life. Many dog owners have found pet insurance to be extremely worthwhile – all too many have only thought about taking out a policy once disaster has struck.

4. Medical care

Most owners will first take their dog to the vet as a puppy for its vaccinations and general health check. Just as children tend to spend more time at the doctor's surgery than adults, puppy owners tend to pay quite frequent visits to their vet. Usually this settles down to just the annual booster vaccinations and an occasional problem visit thereafter. As your dog gets older, problems again become more common, and it is to your advantage to build up a good working relationship with a veterinary surgeon so that the vet gets to know your pet, and you get to know your vet.

FIRST, FIND A VET

So how should you go about finding a good practice? Many people simply use the vet who is closest to them, and there is certainly something to be said in favour of choosing a vet who is close to hand when needed, particularly if your dog is a bad traveller. The surgeries in your area will be listed in British Telecom's Yellow Pages and the Thomson Directory under 'Veterinary Surgeons and Practitioners'.

But, there are other considerations, and first and foremost you will need to find someone who seems to care about your dog and who inspires your confidence. The facilities that are available for treatment are also important – the waiting-room should be clean and tidy, the staff friendly and well-trained, and the surgery should have modern equipment such as X-rays, gaseous anaesthesia and hospitalisation facilities. The Royal College of Veterinary Surgeons publishes a directory of veterinary practices, and those conforming to the recommended standards laid down by the British Small Animal Veterinary Association are marked accordingly – the directory should be available for inspection at any public library.

The British Veterinary Hospital Association lays down even more stringent regulations regarding the premises, equipment and nursing care available, and only practices conforming to these guidelines are allowed to describe themselves as 'Veterinary Hospitals'. All practices are ethically obliged to offer a 24-hour emergency service to their clients, although in some cases this may involve a rota with other neighbouring practices or with a central emergency clinic in the area.

Recommendation from a reliable friend is an excellent means of selecting a practice, although at the end of the day there is no substitute for going along and trying one out. Once you have found a practice that suits you, do not chop and change. If you are not happy with the results of a particular course of treatment, discuss it with the veterinary surgeon caring for your dog.

If you still can not see the way forward, ask your vet to arrange for a referral to a specialist for that particular type of problem. This is far preferable to just turning up at another veterinary surgery and expecting another vet to take over the case. Veterinary surgeons are not permitted to do this without first obtaining the permission of the vet who has already been treating the patient. More importantly, too, for the sake of the animal, it is also vital to have full details of all diagnostic tests and treatments that have been carried out already.

Getting to the vet

Most vets discourage house calls when possible, as it is much more difficult to examine and treat a dog properly without all the correct equipment and trained staff to hand. It also takes up a great deal more of the vet's time and therefore is much more expensive for you. Find out before your visit about how the consultations are organised. Many surgeries now operate an appointment system, and this should avoid long delays in the waiting room. If you think your dog may be suffering from a highly contagious problem, such as kennel cough, let the receptionist know this when you make your appointment so that suitable arrangements can be made to keep your dog away from others. If possible, give your dog a chance to stretch his legs and empty his bladder before you visit the surgery. If your dog is untrustworthy, it might be best to put on a muzzle whilst he is relaxed and before he gets into the surgery. Sometimes a vet will prescribe sedatives for a very nervous dog to make examination easier, although the dog will have to be checked over first to make sure there are no underlying problems that might be aggravated by the drugs.

WHEN TO SEEK VETERINARY HELP

Although some lucky dogs may go through life without the need for any special or emergency veterinary care, most will need help at some point, especially as the years march on. Just how well they recover or cope with problems can be entirely dependent on the speed with which their owners first notice the problem and then act to do something about it. This fast action is important throughout the dog's life but never more so than in old age. It is then that problems begin to occur in multiples – the younger pet probably had one thing wrong with it at a time, while the older animal may have several interacting problems, complicating the illness further.

Just as human doctors now specialise in medical care for the elderly, veterinary surgeons are realising the importance of carefully examining each old dog for its own unique set of problems. They must examine all the body's systems, not just the obvious and presenting complaint. What they must also do is to separate the disease problem from the natural ageing process.

Illness isn't the end

Many owners fear that if they take an unfit or ailing dog to their vet that he or she will advise euthanasia because of 'age', not because of the problem. This is now certainly not the case, and recent advances in veterinary care mean that many previously fatal diseases can be tackled successfully. Even if the problem is not curable, much can be done to slow down its progression and give the dog many more painfree and comfortable weeks, or even years, to enjoy with its family.

Preventative medicine

Prevention is always better than cure. This cannot be said often enough. Booster vaccinations should be kept up throughout the life of a dog, not only to maintain protection against disease but also to allow the veterinary surgeon an opportunity to give the dog a health examination.

Senior pet programmes

Many vets are now taking the role of prevention further by offering clients the chance to arrange for their dog to have a regular health screen in order to try and pick up disease problems early – often before the owner is really aware that a problem exists. A typical 'senior pet programme' would include the following items:

- Thorough physical examination
- Discussion of diet and lifestyle
- Blood test
- Urine examination
- Further tests, such as X-rays and ECGs if necessary.

There is no reason why this sort of in-depth health screening should not be carried out at any age, but most vets would recommend that it is carried out, on at least an annual basis, from around the age of 8 years, or younger for the giant breeds. Dogs are extremely good at masking signs of any problems until they become quite advanced, but it is rare not to turn up at least one minor problem in a dog of that age, such as early dental disease or the first signs of kidney problems. In some cases, potentially very serious problems can be diagnosed and treated much more effectively than if the owner had waited until the dog showed obvious signs of distress.

Advanced anaesthetics

Anaesthetics are now much safer than they were twenty or thirty years ago, and it is now not unusual to carry out operations on even the most elderly of dogs. While veterinary surgeons will not wish to carry out procedures under anaesthetic that are not entirely necessary for an older dog, age itself is no longer a contraindication for anaesthesia. Very effective sedatives that can be reversed once the operation is completed are now also available to use for some minor procedures. If a problem is causing pain or discomfort or is likely significantly to shorten the lifespan of the dog if left untreated, then an operation may well be the best course of action. If your dog is suffering from a particular condition that may increase the anaesthetic risks, such as heart disease, the veterinary surgeon may well try to treat the problem medically beforehand. Each case has to be decided on the individual merit, and you should be guided by your veterinary surgeon on the decision of whether or not to operate.

HEALTH CHECKS TO MAKE AT HOME

Check over your dog regularly. It is amazing how many owners accept their animals as part of the furnishings and never really physically examine them. If you own a long-haired dog, you will probably have been in the habit of grooming it regularly throughout its life, and this is an ideal time to check that all is well. Watch for any changes in your dog's daily habits as well. An observant owner will quickly spot signs of illness such as difficulty in urinating, blood in urine or faeces, excessive straining to pass a motion, or an increase in drinking. It only takes a minute or two to give your dog a once-over.

Physical checkpoints

EARS Any abnormal discharge or soreness may indicate infection or ear-mite infestation. Long-eared dogs are particularly prone to ear infections, and an abnormal smell from the ear is often the first sign of impending disease.

EYES Look for signs of soreness or abnormal discharge. A slight watery discharge may be normal, especially in some of the flat-nosed breeds, but there should not be a thick discharge. Many older dogs develop a cloudiness of the lens, situated behind the pupil, due to cataract development. This often only develops very slowly but in some cases can lead to blindness (*see* chapter 5).

NOSE Again look for any abnormal discharges. If the dog has a pink, unpigmented nose, then a change in colour, such as pallor (*see* anaemia, chapter 5), may be noticeable. Some older dogs develop a crustiness and cracking of the pigmented skin of the nose that may require treatment if it becomes sore.

INSIDE THE MOUTH Check for any ulcers or soreness in the throat or on the tongue, or soreness of the gums, which may be caused by an accumulation of calculus (tartar) on the teeth – a brown discolouration of the teeth caused by a light accumulation of tartar may not be of any significance if it is not yet affecting the gums. Bad breath (halitosis) can be an indication of either a dental problem or of some more generalised disease such as kidney failure and should be reported to your vet.

COAT Check for any sores, scabs, loss of hair or general scurfiness and poor coat quality. You may be able to see signs of external parasites such as fleas – very often you will not spot the fleas themselves, but the reddish-brown flea dirt that they leave behind (it is actually dried blood and will form a reddish-brown halo if put on to a piece of damp cotton wool). Fleas need to be tackled both on the dog and in the house. Most dogs suffer from cat fleas, and all cats and dogs in the household must be treated.

BODY Feel the body for any unusual lumps or bumps. Particularly check the mammary tissue in a bitch and feel the testicles for any unusual swellings in a male dog (but warm your hands first!).

PAWS Check the nails in case they have become overgrown (*see* overgrown nails, chapter 5). Infections between the skin under the toes is quite common.

UNDER THE TAIL Look under the tail for any swelling around the anus, such as that caused by anal adenoma growths in elderly male dogs (*see* chapter 5). Impaction of the anal sacs (scent glands found either side of the anus) can occur at any age and they may require emptying.

BREATHING Watch the normal breathing pattern of your dog. Respiratory problems are quite common in elderly dogs, and the first sign could be laboured breathing even when the dog is relaxed and at rest. With more severe chest problems, the whole pattern of respiration may change, with the dog using its abdominal muscles to try and push air in and out of its chest.

Behavioural checkpoints

You should also watch out for any changes in your dog's behaviour pattern. Most owners are very attuned to the normal routine of their own dog and get the feeling that something is not quite right before there are any obvious signs of illness. Behavioural changes that could be of particular significance are listed here:

DIFFICULTY IN URINATING Can be due to an infection of the bladder, or some form of obstruction to the flow of urine. Leaking of urine after lying down can indicate a hormonal deficiency.

AN INCREASED THIRST This is a sign that can be an important indicator of several common diseases in the elderly dog. Check roughly how much you have to top up the drinking bowl each day.

ASKING TO GO OUT MORE OFTEN This could indicate that the dog is suffering from diarrhoea or cystitis (*see* chapter 5: cystitis; digestive upsets), or that the dog is drinking more than normal and simply unable to hold in the urine.

CHANGE IN EATING PATTERNS Any change in eating or a loss of appetite for more than a day or two can signal illness. Some dogs are finicky eaters anyway and often skip meals, whereas some owners can set their watches by their dogs' demanding food. It is the change in the pattern that is normal for your dog, which is important. You may also be able to detect that your dog has a sore mouth by the way that it eats the food once picked out of the bowl.

DECREASED EXERCISE TOLERANCE If your dog seems to tire on a walk with which he used to cope effortlessly, this can be an indication of cardiac or circulatory problems.

Seek advice

If you are in any way concerned about the health of your dog, get veterinary advice. The vet is there to help you and should be only too happy to check a problem early on and hopefully put your mind at rest. The earlier any problem is identified, the more chance there is of it being easily corrected. There is a tremendous amount that can be done with modern veterinary medicine to cure or control many problems, which were until recently untreatable.

Collecting a sample

A urine sample can be very useful for the diagnosis of many problems in elderly dogs, particularly those that cause the dog to drink more than normal. Specialised urine bottles that attach to collecting funnels can be purchased from your vet, but it is perfectly in order to use a saucer to catch the urine and then transfer it into a clean bottle. It is particularly important to wash out the bottle very thoroughly if it has contained anything sweet, as any sugar left in the bottle could produce a false diagnosis of diabetes. Get a helper to take the dog out on a lead, and be ready to slip the saucer underneath the dog once the flow of urine commences. You may have to be very quick indeed with a male dog, who saves little squirts for every lamp post in the district. You don't need to collect a large volume of urine – a couple of teaspoonfuls will do, but it does have to be uncontaminated and fresh. Keep it in a cool place if you have to store it for any length of time.

NURSING A SICK DOG

While your dog may well need to be hospitalised at your vet's surgery for an operation or intensive nursing care, dogs generally thrive best in familiar surroundings. Therefore your veterinary surgeon will probably be eager to return your dog to you as soon as possible. It is thus essential that you are clear about any specific directions that are given to you, and you should not hesitate to contact the surgery if you are unclear in any way. Administering medicines reliably is also extremely important – but sometimes easier said than done. The following guidelines should help you:

Dealing with wounds

If your dog has had an operation, there is a strong chance that it will have a sutured wound. The stitches may be uncovered, and the dog is bound to lick at the wound. This does not usually do any harm, but if any stitches do come loose, however, you should closely supervise the dog to try and prevent any more from being removed and visit the vet at the earliest opportunity. If the wound is gaping open it may well have to be resutured, so do not give your dog a meal before you visit the surgery in case a general anaesthetic has to be given.

In some cases it is necessary to fit the dog with an Elizabethan collar, a wide plastic cone that fits over the neck and physically prevents the dog from worrying at a wound whilst still letting it eat and drink. These are not particularly popular with dogs, especially when they first go on, but most dogs eventually get used to them after a day or two. Bandages or plasters should be kept clean and dry (waterproof dog socks are available for use on walks). If you notice an unpleasant smell, a lot of swelling, or if the dog seems particularly uncomfortable, you should have the wound checked.

Follow your vet's advice about exercise, which may need to be severely restricted after some orthopaedic operations.

Administering medicines

EAR DROPS Any dirt and wax should be gently cleaned from the ear. Hold the ear flap and use a cotton-tipped stick, but do not insert it deeper than the depth of the cotton tip. Then, keeping hold of the ear flap firmly, allow the drops to drip into the ear canal – the dog may resent it less if you warm the bottle of drops in your hand first. Hold on to the ear flap long enough to allow the drops to run down deep into the ear. Clean away any excess ointment.

EYE DROPS Hold the nose of the dog with one hand, and approach with the bottle or tube from above. Either allow a drop to fall on to the surface of the eye, or pull the lower lid downward and put a small amount of ointment between the lower eyelid and the eye. Do not touch the surface of the eye with the bottle or tube, and do not allow the end of the bottle or tube to become contaminated.

TABLETS Grasp the lower jaw with one hand and the upper jaw with the other. Pull the mouth open and squeeze the upper lips over the upper teeth to prevent the dog from shutting its mouth again. Quickly push the tablet right to the back of the throat and hold the dog's mouth shut until you are sure it has been swallowed. Alternatively, pop the pill into a piece of cheese or titbit and the dog will have gulped it down before he knows it!

LIQUID MEDICINES Hold the mouth shut and the head tilted well back. Lift the flap of the upper lip and slowly pour the medicine between a gap in the dog's teeth (or from a dropper) so that it runs to the back of the dog's throat. Do not administer it too quickly, or the dog may inhale the medicine.

5. Ailments in older dogs: an A-Z

The following chapter outlines the diseases that are most common in the older dog. The chart overleaf will help you find the right part of the chapter if you are concerned about the health of your dog. By referring to the signs of illness on the left and answering the questions along the route, you will be guided to the section which is most likely to be relevant to your dog's illness. This is only a guide and is not a substitute for a proper veterinary examination. For your dog's sake, do not hesitate to obtain proper veterinary advice if you are worried about its health.

ANAL ADENOMAS

These are growths which are common around the anus of elderly male dogs. They develop under the influence of male hormones. They are not usually cancerous, but can become quite large and often bleed profusely. Individual growths can be surgically removed or frozen with liquid nitrogen so that they die and drop off. Hormone treatment can be given to prevent them from recurring, but the long-term cost and the likelihood of side-effects makes surgical castration a preferable alternative in all but the most frail of dogs.

ARTHRITIS

Arthritis is an inflammation of the joints. In old age it commonly takes the form of degenerative osteoarthritis (a chronic arthritis in which the joints deteriorate), and results in swelling, pain and stiffness in the joints. The cause may relate back to some problem earlier in life such as hip dysplasia or osteochondritis dissecans (*see* chapter 3), which caused some damage to one or more joints and has then set up a degenerative arthritis in later life. Earlier injuries, such as torn ligaments, may also trigger the disease, but in many cases

What is the matter with my dog?

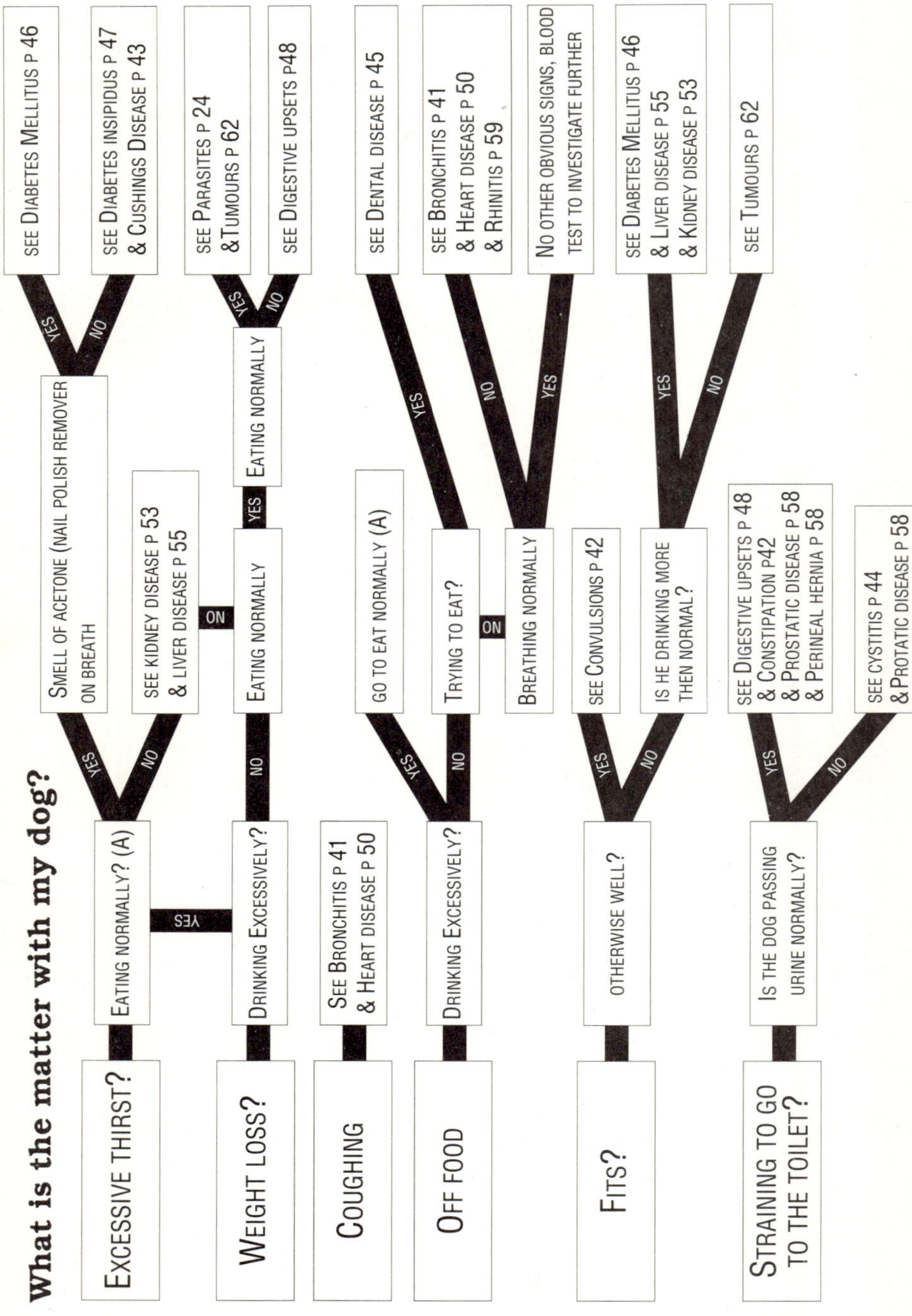

the underlying cause is simply not known. Certain breeds, such as the Labrador Retriever, seem to be particularly prone to the condition. They are also prone to obesity, which puts more strain on to the joints, and a strict weight control programme is often essential.

An owner will often notice lameness, particularly after first getting up from lying down for any length of time, and an unwillingness to jump or go for long walks. The dog may sometimes cry out in pain, or simply refuse to get up at all. Like most humans, dogs tend to suffer more when the weather is cold and damp. X-rays of the affected joints may be needed to confirm the diagnosis.

Surgical treatment of any underlying bone problem is only rarely helpful in the older dog, but medical treatment can play a very useful role in controlling the condition. The most common form of treatment is with NSAIDs (non-steroidal anti-inflammatory drugs), which reduce the pain and swelling in the joints. Whilst many dogs can remain on these drugs for years without problems, other may suffer from side-effects, particularly vomiting or diarrhoea, although this can be minimised by giving medication with food. Aspirin and phenylbutazone ('bute') are two of the more old-fashioned drugs that are nevertheless quite effective and still widely used, but more modern NSAIDs have been developed to maximise the effect and minimise any adverse reactions – but unfortunately at a greater cost. It is worth working together with your vet to discover which of this range of drugs suits your dog best. Just a word of warning about giving your pet human medications, which can often be risky. Ibuprofen is a safe NSAID in humans that is widely available from pharmacists (for example, as Nurofen), but in dogs it can cause very severe stomach ulceration with only a relatively small dose, so do check with your vet before trying out any proprietary medicines.

The more severe cases of osteoarthritis are often treated with corticosteroid anti-inflammatory drugs, such as prednisolone, and some tablets contain this drug in combination with other anti-inflammatories. The effect of these corticosteroids is often dramatic, but their effectiveness is also matched by an increase in possible side-effects, which initially include an increase in thirst and appetite, but in the long term can result in the development of muscle wasting, hair loss, secondary infections and even diabetes mellitus and Cushing's disease (*see* pp.43 - 4). Despite this, the decision is often made that it is better to keep an elderly dog comfortable on this type of drug for a shorter time, than to let the dog live a longer lifespan in misery. The side-effects can be minimised by keeping the dog on the lowest dose possible to control the arthritis, preferably given every alternate day rather than daily. Once a dog has been on corticosteroidal treatment for any length of time, the treatment should not be abruptly stopped or the dog may collapse.

A relatively new product is showing considerable promise for older dogs suffering from arthritis. Pentosan polysulphate sodium is a prescription drug known as Cartrophen Vet in the UK. It works by helping the damaged cartilage to re-form within the affected joints, so helping to reverse the condition rather than just cover up the effects. The drug is initially given by injection on a weekly basis for four weeks, and can then be repeated monthly to keep the arthritis under control.

Because of the chronic and basically incurable nature of degenerative osteoarthritis, many proprietary pet remedies that claim to help with the condition are available. Cod liver oil is often recommended, although care must be taken to avoid over-dosage as it contains very large amounts of Vitamin A that can be harmful in excess. Rhus tox is the homoeopathic remedy most commonly used for this condition, although a wide range of homoeopathic remedies are available. It is best to ask your own vet to refer you to a vet that specialises in complementary medicine to match the correct remedy to your pet . A herbal infusion of comfrey, or fresh garlic crushed with the food have also been recommended, and some owners resort to the use of copper bracelets, although keeping them in place on a dog can be rather more difficult than with a human. Unfortunately, none of these alternative remedies seem to be very effective against arthritis, despite the claims of their manufacturers. Careful weight control, regular but gentle exercise and protection from the cold seem to be the most effective means of keeping your dog comfortable, backed up by drug treatment when necessary (*see* also chapter 9).

BACK PAIN

Back pain is particularly common in dogs with an excessively long back, such as Dachshunds and Corgis, where degenerative osteoarthritis of the joints between the vertebrae and even prolapse of an intervertebral disc is common (*see* also under 'paralysis'). The intervertebral discs consist of an outer fibrous ring and an inner gelatinous material that act as cushioning pads between the bones of the spine. In middle-aged and older dogs the outer ring sometimes degenerates and the semi-fluid disc material is squeezed out (prolapses) from between the vertebrae and pushed onto the nerves of the spine itself. If a lot of new bone is formed between the vertebrae (a condition known as spondylitis), they can sometimes fuse together. Degenerative disease of the spine is most common in the mid-lumbar, or middle, region of the back. It can also affect the neck, when it causes acute pain and stiffness, or in the lumbosaccral region at the base of the spine, when it can cause hindlimb signs that can be very similar to those caused by arthritis in the hip joints.

Severe cases of back pain caused by a disc problem are sometimes treated with an operation to remove the affected disc and relieve the pressure on the spine, but unless signs of paralysis are developing, it is more common to treat the condition medically. Anti-inflammatory drugs will often help the dog to recover, but strict rest is absolutely essential, and there is a danger that the use of pain killing drugs will encourage the dog to exercise more and further injure the spine. Just as with arthritis, obesity can play a major role in aggravating back problems, and a weight control programme may be necessary, particularly if exercise has to be restricted.

BLINDNESS

Blindness is not uncommon in older dogs. It may result from a hereditary eye disease such as progressive retinal atrophy (PRA) (*see* chapter 3), that has been gradually developing since birth. Most dogs show signs of some cloudiness of the lens (situated just behind the pupil), as they age. Sometimes this cloudiness progresses into fully developed cataracts that cause blindness. Other causes of blindness in older dogs include glaucoma (a build-up of pressure within the globe of the eye), or chronic scarring of the cornea (the front surface of the eye), which may lose its normal transparency and become opaque. Diseases affecting other parts of the body can also affect the eye – for example, sometimes cancerous blood cells caused by leukaemia can settle in the eye; or an increased blood pressure can cause detachment of the light-sensitive retina at the back of the eye.

Of course, if possible, the underlying cause of the blindness should be identified and treated. There are now many specialist veterinary ophthalmic surgeons who are able to carry out very sophisticated operations, such as the removal of cataracts and the surgical treatment of glaucoma. If an underlying disease is affecting the eye, then the treatment of that problem can often result in an improvement in vision. Unfortunately, there is often nothing that can be done when blindness does develop in an elderly dog. For example, cataracts are often associated with a degeneration of the retina, and there is no point in removing the affected lens surgically if the retina at the back of the eye is not detecting the images properly anyway.

Elderly dogs do tend to adapt to blindness very well, particularly if it develops slowly. Their sense of smell is far more sensitive than ours, and they are able to follow tracks and recognise people without needing their sense of sight. Many blind dogs can live a nearly normal life for many years, exercising on a flexible lead to ensure their owner has some control over their movements, and learning their way around the house – provided the furniture isn't moved around too often! (*see also* chapter 9).

BRONCHITIS

Bronchitis is an inflammation of the air passages within the lungs, and is a very common cause of coughing in older dogs. An X-ray is often needed to confirm the diagnosis, ruling out other causes such as heart disease and lung tumours. Sometimes the response to a course of antibiotics can be excellent, but with many cases of chronic bronchitis, antibiotics have little effect. It is then necessary to give symptomatic treatment to help control the cough. The most common drugs used are the theophylline group, derived from the stimulant found in tea and used to dilate the airways, remove fluid, and mildly stimulate the heart. The trade names of these drugs include Theocardin, Millophylline and Corvental, the latter prepared in a slow-release capsule form that only has to be given once a day. Cough suppressants may also be given in some cases, although they can encourage the build-up of phlegm within the chest that coughing would normally bring up. As with many 'old dog' problems, obesity can aggravate the condition.

CANCER – *SEE* TUMOURS

CONSTIPATION

Constipation is a difficulty in passing motions, and should be differentiated from simply not needing to pass motions for a period of time, such as after a period of not eating. It is also important not to confuse straining due to constipation with straining to pass urine, as the latter could indicate a blockage to the urinary tract which must be dealt with as an emergency. The most common cause of constipation is motions which are too hard to be passed easily, such as happens when the dog is on a very low fibre diet. It can be particularly common in dogs that crunch up bones. The fragments of bone in the faeces may make them very hard, or sometimes a splinter of bone digs into the lining of the rectum and causes the dog severe pain when it tries to pass a motion. Constipation can also be caused by some external mass pushing onto the rectum and narrowing the passage. This can be caused by an enlargement of the prostate gland (*see* prostatic disease) in male dogs. Polyps within the pelvis or a narrowing of the bones of the pelvic canal itself following a fracture can also cause problems.

A dose of liquid paraffin is often all that is required to cure a mild case of constipation, and the problem can often be avoided by adding extra roughage such as wheat bran, to the diet. Special granules are also available that absorb water into the bowel and soften the faeces. In severe cases of constipation it may be necessary for a vet to administer an enema under sedation or even general anaesthesia to evacuate the bowel.

CONVULSIONS

Convulsions are also known as 'fits' or seizures. A dog with convulsions will usually lose consciousness, fall onto the ground, paddle with its legs and salivate profusely. In partial seizures the dog may not lose consciousness. This is usually very distressing for the owner to watch, although the dog is not actually aware of what is happening. There is very little that can be done whilst a dog is having a convulsion, other than to put it in a dark and quiet room away from anything which is likely to cause injury. Do not try to pull out the dog's tongue or open its mouth – there is no danger of the dog swallowing its tongue but there is a real risk of getting bitten. If the convulsion carries on unabated for more than ten minutes you should seek veterinary attention without further delay. Even if the dog seems to return back to normal after a fit ends, it is still wise to have a full examination carried out to try and identify the cause.

Convulsions can be caused by a problem within the brain itself, or by some disorder elsewhere in the body that affects the brain. Epilepsy is the most common cause in young dogs, but is much less likely to commence once a dog gets older. Unfortunately, brain tumours are not uncommon in older dogs, and distemper virus can cause fits in old dogs as well as young. Both liver and kidney disease can affect the brain and trigger off fits. Although one would hope that an elderly dog would be too wise to ingest poison, this is certainly not always the case, and a wide range of poisons such as strychnine and some rodenticides can cause convulsions.

A clinical examination and a careful consideration of the medical history of the dog will help to identify any underlying causes of the fits, and a blood test may well assist. The diagnosis of disorders within the brain itself can be very difficult, as abnormalities may not show up in the blood, and X-rays do not give much information about the soft tissues of the brain enclosed within the bony case of the skull. Brain scanners are beginning to be used in veterinary medicine, although their cost restricts their use to just one or two referral centres at the present time.

If the cause can be established and treated, the dog may cease to have the convulsions. Special diets help in cases of liver or kidney disease (*see* pp.67 - 8), and if a dog recovers from the effects of a bout of poisoning, the problem is unlikely to recur once that poison is removed.

CUSHING'S DISEASE

Cushing's disease is a strange name, yet considerably easier to pronounce than its more strictly correct scientific name, hyperadrenocorticalism. It most commonly affects middle-aged and older dogs, particularly small Terriers, Poodles, Cavalier King Charles Spaniels and Boxers. The disease is caused by an over-active adrenal gland. This is a small gland situated close to each kidney that produces corticosteroid drugs. It is actually the outer layer (the cortex) that produces these steroid hormones, and the overproduction that occurs in this disease is caused by either a tumour in the adrenal cortex itself, or much more commonly, due to a tumour in the pituitary gland (the 'master gland' situated at the base of the brain, responsible for producing hormones that control several other glands around the body). In the case of the adrenal cortex, it produces a hormone called adrenocortical stimulating hormone (ACTH), and excessive levels of this in blood cause the adrenal cortex to produce excessive amounts of corticosteroids and thus the signs of Cushing's disease.

The most pronounced signs of Cushing's disease are an increased thirst and an increased appetite, usually accompanied by wasting of the muscles and enlargement of the liver, which in combination cause the dog to develop a marked pot-belly appearance. Dogs also often develop a thinning of the coat over the flanks, which can gradually spread to cause baldness over much of the body. A tumour within the pituitary gland itself may only grow very slowly, but it can cause pressure upon the rest of the brain and cause neurological signs as head pressing (literally pressing the head against walls), confusion and even convulsions.

In order to diagnose the disease it is necessary to measure the cortisone levels in the blood both before and a couple of hours after an injection of ACTH. Treatment is not straightforward, but it is possible to administer a drug called mitotane that kills off tissue in the adrenal cortex and thus lowers its output of steroid hormone. This drug is not licensed for use in dogs, and has to be specially ordered for each case to be treated. It is fairly expensive, and side-effects are not uncommon. Despite all these problems, quite a lot of elderly dogs with this condition are treated and maintained on regular doses of this drug. In cases caused by a tumour of the adrenal cortex itself, surgical removal of that tumour is possible, but technically very difficult to carry out.

CYSTITIS

Cystitis is an inflammation of the bladder which is more common in bitches than dogs and can strike at any time of life. It is most often caused by a bacterial infection, with the bugs that cause the problem normally being found lower down the urinary tract, but travelling up the urethra into the bladder when the body's normal defences against infection are below par. It is also possible for stones to form within the bladder from crystalline matter passed in the urine, or for growths to develop.

Signs of cystitis or other problems affecting the bladder usually include an increased frequency of urination, discomfort and straining on passing the urine, and possibly blood or pus in the urine itself. Examination of a urine sample is an essential part in the diagnosis of this condition and cases that do not respond to treatment with antibiotics often require further specialised tests such as X-rays and possibly ultrasound examination to try and determine the cause.

Many cases of cystitis respond well to antibiotic treatment but tend to recur. Keeping up the water intake of the dog helps to flush out bacteria from the bladder. You can achieve this by making sure a supply of fresh water is readily available at all times, adding some water to the food, or adding some salt into the diet (but not if the dog has had any heart problems). Many dogs with recurrent cystitis produce an excessively alkaline urine, and giving substances to acidify the urine can also be effective as a long-term control measure, but this should only be done under veterinary supervision.

DEAFNESS

Our survey of older dogs showed deafness to be a common problem in dogs over 10 years of age, affecting about 10 per cent at that age, rising to 45 per cent in 14-year-olds and over 60 per cent of the over-15s. It can be rather difficult to be sure if your dog is just becoming stubborn and ignoring you in his old age, or whether deafness genuinely is a problem. The only way to scientifically measure hearing ability in dogs is with sophisticated electronic equipment under general anaesthesia, but most owners notice that the dog fails to hear certain noises to which it normally reacts such as doorbells, or the opening of a can of food at feeding time. Owners often think this may be due to an ear infection, or the build-up of wax within the ear canal, but this is very rarely the case. Far more commonly, deafness is simply due to a degeneration of the hearing apparatus deep within the inner ear that comes with old age. Unfortunately, hearing aids for dogs are quite some way off yet! (*see* also chapter 9 for tips).

DENTAL DISEASE

Bad teeth were mentioned in our survey far more than any other problem, confirming the results of surveys that have shown that about two-thirds of older dogs that visit veterinary surgeries have some degree of dental disease. It is unusual for dogs to suffer from dental decay, or caries, in the same way as humans, unless they are fed on large amounts of sweet foods. Physical injury to the teeth such as chewing on hard bones or even stones may crack the teeth and allow infection to track up into the roots. More commonly, hard calculus build-up on the teeth is formed from minerals deposited from the saliva over the years, along with softer tartar from food particles. This pushes on the gums, causing gingivitis (gum disease), and eventually causing them to recede. A pocket or space then forms in the area around the base of the tooth and encourages bacterial infection into the structure which binds the tooth into its bony socket. Eventually, either an abscess forms above the tooth root, or the tooth loosens in its socket and falls out.

A light deposition of brown tartar on the teeth is of no great significance unless it is causing a reddening of the gums, indicating that gingivitis is developing. Many owners of elderly dogs with dental disease notice that their pet suffers from bad breath, and on examining the mouth discover that the gums are sore and inflamed. The dog may rub its mouth along the ground, paw at its mouth, or have obvious difficulty in eating. If an abscess forms on a tooth root, you may notice a painful swelling, especially below the eye if one of the large upper carnassials is affected (known as a malar abscess). The roots of the upper canine teeth are very long and extend well up into the area around the nose, so inflammation around these roots can cause a nasal discharge and sneezing, as well as a swelling of the tissues around the muzzle. If gingivitis is caught in the early stages, it may be possible to remove the accumulated tartar by commencing a programme of regular brushing with dog toothpaste and thus prevent any further deterioration of the condition (*see* chapter 3 for more detailed information on preventative dental care).

The main treatment for dental disease involves administering a general anaesthetic, extracting any teeth with badly infected roots and descaling the others. Sometimes it is necessary to X-ray the teeth to examine the health of the roots. Descaling it usually carried out with an ultrasonic dental scaler which uses a jet of water vibrating at high speed to loosen the hard calculus without damaging the teeth. This is followed by polishing to ensure the surfaces of the teeth are left smooth so that they will not rapidly attract further deposits. If deep pockets have formed in the gums around some of the teeth, the unattached gum may need to be cut away to prevent food from accumulating. The earlier the condition is treated, the more chance there is of avoiding the need for extractions.

Medical preparations are often used in conjunction with this dental care to clear away any infection and try to slow down any recurrence of the problem. Antibiotic treatment may be necessary and, if the dog is co-operative, oral antiseptic solutions can be painted onto the gums. Once the tartar has been removed, regular brushing is essential if at all possible, although there are now enzymatic dental preparations to help disperse the calculus and tartar that can just be applied topically to the teeth and do not need brushing. Ask your vet or veterinary nurse to show you the areas that need special attention, and how to cope with oral hygiene.

DIABETES MELLITUS

Diabetes mellitus is also known as sugar diabetes, because it results in a build-up of glucose in the blood and in the urine. It is quite common in dogs over eight years of age, and is three times more common in females than males. Breeds most commonly affected include the Dachshund, Miniature Poodle and Scottish Terrier. The tendency to develop diabetes is to some extend hereditary, but is also influenced by treatment with certain drugs such as corticosteroids and progesterone-type hormones, and by obesity. As Cushing's disease (*see* Cushings disease) also causes elevated levels of corticosteroids in the blood, it can also predispose to the development of diabetes.

Insulin is a hormone produced by the pancreas, an organ situated along the border of the upper small intestine, that is responsible for regulating the levels of glucose in the blood by controlling the breakdown of carbohydrates. Diabetes mellitus can be caused either by an under-production of insulin by the pancreas, or a failure of the body to react correctly to the insulin that is being produced. Since the body is unable to utilise carbohydrates as an energy source properly, it increases the breakdown of fats, resulting in a build-up of poisonous waste products known as ketones in the blood. Despite a ravenous appetite and thirst, diabetic animals lose weight because of their inability to use the food they are eating properly, and it may be possible to detect the smell of ketones on the breath – a sweetish smell rather like nail polish remover. About 25 per cent of diabetic dogs develop cataracts (*see* Blindness). The build-up of poisons within the body causes liver damage, and if left untreated a diabetic dog will lapse into a coma and die. The diagnosis of diabetes mellitus can be simply made by testing a urine or blood sample.

Fortunately, diabetes mellitus in the dog can usually be controlled very effectively by daily doses of insulin. This has to be given by injection because the oral drugs given to help reduce blood glucose levels in humans can be quite toxic to dogs. Initially, the dog has to be given gradually increasing doses of insulin to bring the blood glucose levels down, and then the dog has to be maintained on a steady level of insulin to keep the problem under control. This must be carried out under strict veterinary supervision with regular blood or urine tests to monitor the effect because if the blood sugar level drops too low the dog may suffer hypoglycaemic fits. The owner of any dog on insulin treatment should always have some glucose powder available to make up with water and administer at the first sign of low blood sugar levels. The aim is to keep the blood glucose at a level where it just shows as a trace in the urine. This way, the urine can be tested regularly by the owner to ensure that the insulin levels are neither too high or too low.

If the insulin is to be kept at a steady dose, it is essential that the dog receives a very stable routine of food and exercise each day – extra food will raise the blood glucose levels and extra exercise will cause them to drop. Special diets (available from vets), with high soluble fibre levels have been found to be beneficial in avoiding major fluctuations in blood glucose levels.. Despite the daunting prospect of keeping a dog on a regular routine with daily injections for the rest of its life, many owners learn to cope with the treatment extremely well, and diabetic dogs can go on to live for four or five years once the problem has been diagnosed and treated.

DIABETES INSIPIDUS

Not to be confused with diabetes mellitus, diabetes insipidus is rather rarer and is caused by an under-production of a hormone called antidiuretic hormone (ADH) from the pituitary gland in the brain. This hormone regulates the amount of water that is lost by the kidneys, and an under-production results in an inability to concentrate the urine properly. This means that the dog drinks vast volumes of water and voids large quantities of urine, but is otherwise quite well. Diagnosis is less straightforward than with diabetes mellitus, and is carried out by a water deprivation test. This has to be carried out under carefully controlled hospitalised conditions, with regular weighings during the period when water is withdrawn to ensure that the dog does not become excessively dehydrated, because a dog with this condition is totally unable to control its water loss through the kidneys and can rapidly collapse and die if water is witheld for too long. The concentration of the urine is then measured. In a normal dog the urine rapidly becomes more concentrated to make up for the reduced water intake, but in a dog suffering from diabetes insipidus the urine remains very dilute.

Treatment can also present some problems. ADH is available in drop form that can be given into the nose, but it is very expensive and the practicalities of treatment can be insurmountable. Surprisingly, certain diuretics, that normally increase urine output, if given in large doses to dogs suffering from this condition can cause them to drink less. A dog that is left untreated will usually thrive perfectly well providing it is given a ready supply of large quantities of water – the problem is more for the poor owner trying to cope with the vast amounts of urine that are produced!

DIGESTIVE UPSETS

Bouts of vomiting and diarrhoea are common at any age, but as a dog gets older, its digestive system becomes more sensitive. Therefore, although a dog may have been coping with a particular diet perfectly well throughout its life, it may well not be able to digest that same diet in old age. Special diets that are adapted to the needs of elderly dogs are discussed in more detail in chapter 6.

Colitis is an inflammation of the large bowel, and is quite a common chronic problem in older dogs. Stools are generally soft, and are passed more frequently than normal with a great deal of straining. They may be streaked with blood, and are very frequently mixed with mucus. Sometimes it is accompanied by vomiting. A change of diet can often solve this type of problem, with some dogs responding well to a highly digestible diet with very little residue passed in the motions, and others thriving on a diet higher in fibre. Sometimes, medical management is required, and a drug called salazopyrin is commonly used. A course of tablets for a few weeks may cure the problem, but in some cases long-term treatment is required.

Acute bouts of diarrhoea and/or vomiting are usually either caused by an infection, or eating something unwholesome. Vomiting should be treated by witholding food for 24 hours, allowing small amounts to drink little and often, and then gradually re-introducing small amounts of a light diet such as white meat or fish with rice. Veterinary attention should be sought if the vomiting persists for more than 24 hours or if the dog seems to be becoming weak and very much off colour. Diarrhoea should also be treated by witholding food for 24 hours and then feeding a bland diet. It is also quite safe to administer a kaolin preparation. Electrolyte solutions containing glucose and minerals are also available, and can be made up with water and given to drink when food is not to be taken. Diarrhoea is less of an urgent problem than vomiting, as dehydration will not generally occur as rapidly, but veterinary attention should be sought if it persists severely for more than 48 hours, or if there are other worrying signs such as a significant amount of blood in the motions.

EAR INFECTIONS

The shape of the ear of many breeds of dog (a very deep external canal, covered by a pendulant earflap and surrounded by a lot of hair), means that ventilation is often poor and bacteria thrive in the dark, warm and moist conditions deep down in the ear canal and ear infections are very common. This causes reddening of the outer ear, a discharge of wax, a foul smell and intense irritation. If the infection crosses the eardrum it can affect the organ of balance in the inner ear, resulting in deafness and severe incoordination.

Ear infections usually respond

well to treatment with ear drops containing a combination of antibiotic, antifungal and anti-inflammatory agents, although sometimes it is necessary to thoroughly clean out the ear canals before starting treatment. This may require sedation or even general anaesthesia if the ears are very sore. It is important to ensure that the ear drops are administered deep down into the ears, and not just sprinkled around the ear and shaken on to the wallpaper! The veterinary nursing staff at your surgery will show you how to use the drops effectively if you are having problems. Sometimes oral antibiotic and anti-inflammatory drugs are necessary, particularly if the deeper parts of the ear are affected.

Although most ear infections do respond to treatment, there is a tendency for them to recur. Resist the temptation to use an antibiotic preparation in dribs and drabs whenever the dog seems troubled over a period of time, as this will just encourage the development of resistant infections that fail to respond to any treatment. Your vet can supply you with a cleansing solution to use regularly in the ears that does not contain an antibiotic but simply cleans the ear and creates an environment that the bacteria and fungi do not find so enjoyable. In some cases it is necessary to operate on the ear canal, opening it up to allow air to get in and discharge to get out. This operation is called an aural resection, and is more usually carried out in younger dogs rather than the elderly. In severe middle and inner ear infections it is sometimes necessary to surgically drain the inner chambers of the ear and implant an irrigation tube to allow an antibiotic solution to be instilled.

FITS – *SEE* CONVULSIONS

FLATULENCE

A polite name for wind, flatulence is not generally too much of a problem for the dog, but can be a considerable embarrassment for the owner, particularly as some dogs tend to let rip under the dining table during a carefully prepared dinner party. It is caused by an excessive production of gas by the bacteria in the bowel, and can be an indication that the dog is not digesting its food properly. (*see* chapter 6 for recommendations on feeding elderly dogs). Sometimes the addition of a little live (unpasteurised) yoghurt to the diet may help to re-establish a more normal bacterial population in the bowel. Charcoal biscuits can be fed to try and absorb the worst of the noxious smells.

HALITOSIS

Another smelly problem – but this time from the other end of the dog! Halitosis or bad breath can emanate from a problem within the mouth itself, or from the build-up of waste products in the body, particularly in the case of kidney disease. Since dogs will groom the whole of their body with their tongue, smells from elsewhere, such as infected anal sacs under the tail, can be transferred on to the breath. The most common problem which causes bad breath within the mouth is poor dental hygiene resulting in the build-up of tartar and calculus on the teeth (see Chapter 3 for more details on preventative dental care). Ulcers or growths within the mouth may also cause halitosis. Whilst preparations to mask the smell of bad breath can be purchased, it is always preferable to try and identify and treat the underlying cause of the problem wherever possible.

HEART DISEASE

Heart disease is very common in both elderly dogs and elderly humans, but the pattern of disease is very different. The major killer of humans is a 'heart attack' caused by a coronary thrombosis, an obstruction in the arteries supplying the heart muscle caused by a blood clot and aggravated by a build-up of fatty tissue on the wall of the arteries. This condition, known as atherosclerosis, does not occur in dogs. Although dogs may die suddenly from what we call a 'heart attack', the cause will be different to that of a heart attack in humans.

By far the most common cause of heart disease in dogs is a degeneration of the valves within the heart (known as endocardiosis), which results in the gradual onset of heart failure rather than a sudden heart attack. This is particularly common in the Cavalier King Charles Spaniel and some other small breeds such as the Miniature Poodle. Giant breeds of dog such as the Irish Wolfhound and Great Danes are also very prone to cardiomyopathy, a degeneration of the heart muscle itself that goes on to cause an irregular heartbeat.

Many other disease processes can damage the tissue which conducts electrical impulses through the heart muscle and can cause an irregular heartbeat. Sometimes a congenital heart defect may have been present since birth but only cause problems as the dog reaches old age. As is the case with so many diseases of old age, obesity will put an increased strain on the heart and make problems much more likely.

The two most important aids to diagnosing heart problems, a stethoscope and an X-ray machine, are readily available in general practice, and the treatment of common problems such as a faulty heart valve is an everyday matter to the general practitioner. If a valve is not functioning properly, a heart murmur can usually be heard with the stethoscope – a whooshing sound caused by blood travelling against the normal flow of blood through a leaking valve, and abnormalities in the rate and rhythm of the heart can also be heard. X-rays will show if there is any abnormal enlargement to the outline of the heart, perhaps caused by thickening of the heart muscle, or a build-up of fluid in the sac around the heart itself. It can also show if there is an abnormal build-up of fluid on the lungs, or whether other abdominal organs, such as the liver, are enlarged.

More complex heart conditions are often referred to veterinary cardiologists, who will have more specialised diagnostic equipment at their disposal, as well as a wealth of experience with dealing with this type of problem. Sophisticated techniques such as electrocardiograph (ECG) (measuring the electrical impulses within the heart), Doppler ultrasonography (which can use ultrasound scanners to visualise the flow of blood within the heart itself) and echocardiography (which traces an image of the sounds made by the heart) can all be used to help reach a diagnosis and measure the extend of the disease. It is now possible to measure blood pressure in dogs, although this needs much more sophisticated equipment than the considerably simpler procedure carried out in humans with an inflatable cuff on the arm.

The signs associated with heart disease in the dog may vary, but as the heart fails to pump the blood effectively around the body, fluid will tend to accumulate within the chest and the abdomen. The first sign of this is usually a cough, and possible a swollen abdomen. The dog will tire quickly when exercised and, as the disease progresses, may collapse when stressed because insufficient blood reaches the brain. The fluid that builds up within the body tissues makesthe job of the heart in pumping the blood through those tissues even harder, and this in turn aggravates the deterioration in the heart.

There is nothing that can be done to repair the damaged valves or heart muscle in elderly dogs with heart problems, but a lot can be done to reduce the workload on the heart and prolong life expectancy. The first line of treatment in any advanced case of heart disease is the use of diuretics, which remove the excess fluid from the body, so alleviating the cough and reducing the workload on the heart. These can be combined with drugs such as the cardiac glycosides, which have been used in the form of digitalis extracted from the foxglove plant for hundreds of years, but are now available in a more highly purified form and help to restore the normal rhythm of the heart. Drugs to dilate the blood vessels and reduce the resistance to the output of blood from the heart are also sometimes used. As in humans, reducing the salt intake helps to prevent the build-up of fluid, and a low salt diet is useful in even early cases of heart disease (*see* chapter 6). Some cases of an abnormal heart rate, when the heart is beating too slowly, can now be treated by the implantation of a pacemaker under the skin, with a lead running down an artery into the heart.

The outlook for cases of heart disease depend very much on the cause. Some dogs are diagnosed as having a heart murmur as an incidental finding during a health examination. This problem may only deteriorate very slowly, so that the dog can carry on living for years without any signs of a problem. Even once clinical signs of early heart failure develop because of a valvular problem, the condition can often be kept under control with treatment for several years, but a gradual deterioration usually occurs over a period of months. As this happens, the drug doses have to be stepped up and sometimes other drugs added to the treatment, but of course this should only be carried out under veterinary supervision. The outlook for cases of cardiomyopathy is much worse, and most of the giant breeds of dog affected with this condition die within six months of diagnosis, despite treatment.

HYPOTHYROIDISM

Hypothyroidism is quite a common condition of middle-aged and older dogs, especially in large breeds such as Retrievers, Setters, Dobermanns and Boxers. It is caused by an underproduction of thyroid hormone from the thyroid glands situated at the base of the neck. Thyroid hormone controls the metabolic rate of the body, and affected animals tend to be lethargic, overweight, and often show signs of baldness, especially on either side of the flank. A measurement of blood thyroid hormone levels will usually provide a diagnosis, although there is some overlap between healthy dogs that happen to have a blood thyroid level on the low side of normal, and those suffering from hypothyroidism. In these cases it may be necessary to carry out a more complicated test, injecting a drug to stimulate the thyroid glands and measuring what effect this has on blood thyroid hormone levels.

Treatment is quite straightforward, as it is possible to give tablets to replace the thyroid hormone that the body is not producing on its own. Treatment has to be continued permanently to maintain its effect.

INCONTINENCE

Another common condition in older dogs, as demonstrated by our survey, which showed that 20 per cent of dogs over 15 years of age were affected to some degree by this problem. It can be divided into faecal incontinence and urinary incontinence, although some unlucky owners may have a dog that suffers from both. Faecal incontinence is often associated with some form of bowel problem, causing diarrhoea and an increased urgency to pass a motion. If the motions are abnormal then this underlying problem has to be treated (*see* digestive upsets). It can also be caused by a lack of nervous control, usually because of a problem affecting the nerves that travel from the spine to control the process of defecation, and in this case is often associated with urinary incontinence and signs of hindlimb weakness (*see* paralysis). It can also be due to a behavioural problem (*see* chapter 7), or simply senility (*see* senility).

Nervous conditions affecting the control of defecation can also interfere with the control of urination. It is important to distinguish between the dog that is unable to control its urination, and one that is drinking more than normal, so has to be let out more frequently to urinate and will therefore often wet indoors overnight or when left for any length of time. Kidney disease, diabetes mellitus, diabetes insipidus and Cushing's disease are all examples of conditions that are quite common in older dogs and cause an increased thirst. Cystitis (*see* cystitis) is also a common cause of incontinence, and sometimes tumours of the bladder or lower urinary tract occur in older dogs.

Some causes of incontinence are related to the sex of the dog. In spayed bitches, probably the most common cause of urinary incontinence of all is a weakness of the sphincter muscles that control the passage of urine from the bladder. Hormone treatment can be given to tone up these muscles, and the response to treatment is usually very good, although repeated courses or even continual treatment is sometimes necessary. In elderly male dogs, enlargement of the prostate gland can cause a dribbling of urine.

A urine examination is usually an essential test in the diagnosis of incontinence unless the cause is obvious, and in some cases a blood test may also be necessary. Specialised contrast X-rays can also be used to outline the bladder and lower urinary tract to identify any problems, although this usually has to be carried out under an anaesthetic.

Owners of elderly dogs should not just assume that incontinence is inevitable and untreatable, as this is often not the case. Having said this, some cases simply cannot be cured, and a decision has to be made whether to cope with the problem or put the dog to sleep. This depends upon the severity of the incontinence, the general health of the dog, and the tolerance of the owner, but the problems of caring for a chronically incontinent dog are considerable. The smell and damage to furnishings can deter all but the most determined of visitors to the home, and the dog's skin can easily become infected and urine-scalded.

Specialised bedding materials are available (*see* chapter 9), to help cope with the problem by allowing the urine to soak straight through to absorbent paper placed underneath, so that the fabric in contact with the dog stays dry. The dog must be bathed and thoroughly dried regularly, particularly around the rear, and some waterproof agent such as Vaseline applied to protect the skin. In warm weather it is important to keep flies at bay with the use of an insecticide, because if they are allowed to lay eggs on the skin, maggots can hatch out and eat deeply into the tissues. Mild incontinence can often be coped with by the use of appropriate bedding (see chapter 9) and confining the dog to areas that can be easily cleaned, but in severe cases it is usually kindest both for dog and for the owner to have the dog put to sleep.

KIDNEY DISEASE

Kidney disease is 'public enemy number one' to old dogs. A deterioration in kidney function is inevitable as part of the ageing process, but clinical signs of disease do not develop until more than two-thirds of the total kidney mass has been damaged. The most common form of kidney disease in elderly dogs is chronic interstitial nephritis, where the normal kidney gradually becomes replaced by fibrous scar tissue, although kidney tumours are also quite frequently diagnosed. Chronic interstitial nephritis can be caused by many agents that damage the kidneys but often the cause cannot be identified. To some extent it is a natural ageing change in the kidneys, but some dogs develop it to a far more advanced degree than others. Certain poisons, such as ethylene glycol, found in anti-freeze (attractive to dogs because of its sweet taste), can damage the kidneys, as can some drugs. Infections, often low-grade and contracted earlier on in life, can encourage the development of scar tissue in the kidney of the older dog, and it has been speculated that eating a high-protein diet may also take its toll, although this is disputed by some authorities.

The most obvious and earliest sign of chronic kidney disease is almost always an increase in drinking and urine output. As the condition worsens the dog will lose weight, go off its food, possibly develop vomiting and diarrhoea and feel generally unwell due to a build-up of waste products that the kidneys normally eliminate from the body. Excessive amounts of calcium are lost via the damaged kidneys, and phosphorus is retained, resulting in a weakening of the bone. In the end stages of the disease the dog may cease to eat or drink and have convulsions.

Unfortunately, it is not practicable to measure any effects of kidney damage until a considerable proportion of the total kidney tissue has already been damaged, but measures to limit the damage to the kidneys will be much more effective if instigated as early as possible. Blood tests are used to measure blood urea levels (urea is a poison that builds up in the blood when the kidneys are not functioning properly), and blood creatinine levels (creatinine is an enzyme produced within the body that also builds up in the blood when the kidneys are not filtering the blood as effectively as normal). A urine examination may also show if excessive protein is being lost through the kidneys. One of the most sensitive ways to measure the functioning of the kidneys is to compare urea and creatinine levels in both urine and blood samples taken at the same time. Contrast radiographs using a special dye injected into the bloodstream to outline the structure of the kidneys, or ultrasound scanning, are both useful if some structural abnormality such as a cyst or tumour of the kidneys is suspected.

Although the diagnosis of chronic nephritis spells 'the beginning of the end' for an elderly dog, a lot can be achieved with treatment to obtain a good quality of life for several months or even years if the case is diagnosed early enough. The single most important factor in the control of the disease is a special diet (available from your vet) to reduce the protein intake, as many of the effects of kidney disease are caused by a build-up of waste products from protein breakdown in the body, and reducing the intake of phosphorus, as a build-up of this substance can then cause further kidney damage. More information on special diets for dogs with kidney disease can be found in chapter 6. Anabolic steroids can be used to stimulate the appetite and reduce muscle wasting, and a vitamin supplement will replace excess amounts of vitamins lost through the kidneys and help to boost the elderly dog's general well-being. In advanced cases, intravenous fluid therapy, anticonvulsants, and drugs to suppress vomiting may be needed, but the long term outlook for such cases is very bleak indeed, and the owner must consider if such intensive treatment is fair in an elderly dog.

LARYNGEAL PARALYSIS

This is caused by damage to, or degeneration of the laryngeal nerves that are responsible for pulling the vocal cords out of the airway when the dog breathes in. If they are not functioning properly, the vocal cords will flap in the airway as it passes through the larynx and interfere with the flow of air. In mild cases this causes a slight cough and noisy breathing, but in severe cases it can temporarily totally block the flow of air into the lungs and cause the dog to collapse. The cause of the condition is not known, but it seems to occur particularly commonly in elderly Labradors and Golden Retrievers, and is aggravated by obesity. It tends to gradually worsen as the dog ages.

The diagnosis can be confirmed by examining the vocal cords under light anaesthesia to see if they open and close as the dog breathes. A surgical operation can be carried out to tie back the vocal cords out of the airway if the problem is serious enough to warrant it.

LIVER DISEASE

The liver is the powerhouse of the body, processing food that has been absorbed across the intestines to provide all the nutrients that the body needs. Liver disease is a common condition of elderly dogs that can be caused by many different reasons. Chronic infection, a poorly balanced diet, or the ingestion of harmful substances can all take their toll on the liver, which may eventually develop cirrhosis (a replacement of the normal liver tissue with fibrous scar tissue). Diseases affecting other organs, such as heart failure, may affect the flow of blood through the liver and cause damage. Although rare, it is also possible for dogs to develop gall stones, which form in the gall bladder and may block the flow of bile out from the liver. Unfortunately, it is common for tumours to develop in the liver – either primary ones that start to grow in that position, or secondary tumours that spread to the liver from other parts of the body. After the lungs, the liver is the most common site for these secondary cancers.

Dogs with liver disease suffer frequent digestive upsets, often passing very pale and fatty motions, lose weight, drink excessively and generally seem off colour. The liver often enlarges, and fluid may form, resulting in an enlarged and fluid-filled abdominal cavity. This sign is called ascites. The liver produces bile to help digest the food and, if the passage of bile from the liver cells down the bile ducts and into the intestine is blocked, then jaundice will develop. This is a yellow discolouration caused by a build-up of bile in the tissues, and is most obvious in the mouth and particularly in the whites of the eyes.

Blood tests can be used to diagnose liver disease, and sometimes a urine examination will show up excess levels of bile in the urine. Although a blood test will show that liver damage is occurring, it often does not pinpoint the underlying cause. X-rays and ultrasound may give more information about the changes occurring in the liver, but sometimes it is necessary to carry out a minor surgical procedure to examine the liver and take a small biopsy specimen to study.

As with all diseases, treatment should be aimed at alleviating the underlying cause if it can be identified. With serious problems such as cancer of the liver there is often very little that can be done. General supportive treatment includes feeding a low-fat, easily digested diet (*see* chapter 6) and an extra vitamin and mineral supplement. In particular, an amino acid called methionine (one of the building blocks of proteins) can have some effect in stimulating the damaged liver tissue to regenerate. Specific signs such as gastrointestinal upsets and fluid accumulation can be treated appropriately. Unlike the kidneys, a damaged liver is able to regenerate, and the outlook for a dog with liver disease can be quite good if the condition is diagnosed and treated before it becomes too advanced.

LOSS OF BALANCE

Also known as ataxia, loss of balance can be caused either by damage to the organs of balance in the inner ear, or to the part of the brain that controls balance. The most common cause of the former is an infection of the outer ear that travels across the eardrum (for details of treatment see ear infections). The brain can be affected by infections such as meningitis, but in elderly dogs tumours and strokes (see below) are far more common. Although dogs that have lost their balance due to a stroke often get left with a permanent tilt of the head to one side, they generally learn to cope with the disability very well.

OBESITY

Obesity is the commonest of all nutritional problems, it affects about a third of all elderly dogs and can have a marked effect upon their health. Information on preventing obesity is given in chapter 3, and diets to help treat the problem are outlined in chapter 6.

OVERGROWN NAILS

Young dogs are usually able to keep their nails at the correct length by wearing them down when they exercise, particularly if they do some walking on hard ground such as pavements. Older dogs often do not exercise as much, and sometimes develop a splaying of the toes so the nails are not able to wear down as they should. The nails of an elderly dog should be checked regularly, because if they do overgrow, they are prone to either break off and bleed, or grow right round in a circle and back into the pad of the toe. This is an extremely painful condition, and the ingrown nail may then have to be cut back under anaesthetic to prevent undue suffering. Many owners are able to cut their dog's nails themselves, but others prefer to have the veterinary surgery or grooming parlour carry out the task, especially if the nails are darkly pigmented, as it is then difficult to see the pink quick that runs down the centre of the nail and contains the nerve and blood vessel. You should use specialised nail trimmers and leave about an eighth of an inch of nail over the end of the quick (*see also* chapter 9).

PARALYSIS

Paralysis is a loss of function of a part of the body caused by damage to the nerves controlling the muscles of that region. In elderly dogs it generally affects the hindlimbs. It is not usually a painful condition, as the sensory nerves that detect pain and other sensations are generally affected as well. It often starts as an incoordination of the hindlimbs and then can progress gradually to a total paralysis. It is most commonly due either to something causing pressure upon the spine, such as a severely prolapsed intervertebral disc (*see* back pain), arthritic bone, or a tumour. Some breeds are prone to degenerations of the nerves within the spine as they age, particularly German Shepherd Dogs (GSD), that are very often affected by a disease called chronic degenerative radiculomyopathy (CDRM). The cause is not known, although it is suspected that it is hereditary, and it starts with the dog dragging its hindlegs when it walks – the nails on the hind feet often become worn very short because of this. The condition gradually affects the muscles of the hindlimb so that the dog becomes weaker and less able to stand, and eventually leads to incontinence and total paralysis of the hindquarters. Unfortunately there is no treatment that has any appreciable affect upon the course of this disease.

A close physical examination can often tell the vet about the nature of the condition. Sometimes even the site of the lesion causing the problem can be pinpointed by checking the nervous reflexes in the limbs. The clinical signs of CDRM are so typical in the GSD that further tests are not usually necessary and are unlikely to yield any further information, but in other cases the vet may wish to carry out X-rays of the spine. Contrast medium is often injected around the spine to give a myelogram (an X-ray that will show up any region of pressure impinging upon the spinal cord), and magnetic resonance scanners are extremely useful if they are available.

Disc problems may sometimes respond to conservative treatment, but if surgery is to be successful on a dog that is suffering from acute paralysis, it should be carried out without delay. It is now also possible to surgically remove spinal tumours, as many of them are not cancerous. Anti-inflammatory drugs may give a lease of life to a dog with a spinal tumour, and are also very useful if spinal arthritis is causing the problem.

Some cases of paralysis can be controlled or even cured with treatment, but sometimes this is not possible and a decision has to be made whether the patient should be kept alive or euthanased. It is not usually desirable or practicable to keep alive an elderly dog that has totally lost the use of its hind legs, particularly if it is incontinent. Mobility carts (*see* chapter 9) are available, with two wheels and a harness to support the rear of the body, but these are most suitable for younger dogs that have suffered paralysis due to some injury, such as a road accident, and are still able to control their bodily functions. One aid that is useful for the larger dog that is finding it difficult to get up on to its hind legs, is a support sling (*see* chapter 9). This passes under the abdomen of the dog and has a handle on either side that can be used to give an extra helping hand to get the dog on to its feet and possibly help support it while it walks.

PERINEAL HERNIA

A perineal hernia is caused by a weakening of the muscle tissue on one or both sides of the anus, which allows a bulging of internal organs into a sac that forms in that area. This is most commonly a loop of the rectum filled with faeces, but can involve other organs such as the bladder. It only occurs in elderly male dogs, and is usually caused by straining to pass faeces because of an obstruction of an enlarged prostate. The straining damages the muscles in the area around the anus. This then causes further straining, usually to pass motions, but sometimes also to pass urine if the bladder is involved.

Diagnosis is easily confirmed by a rectal examination, and it is usually possible to repair the damaged muscles surgically. There is quite a high risk of the problem recurring, but this is reduced if the dog is castrated, as this causes the prostate to shrink down (*see* below). Faecal softeners should be given permanently to prevent straining and, in mild cases of perineal herniation, the use of these agents alone coupled with treatment for any underlying prostate problem, may allow the dog to cope.

PROSTATIC DISEASE

Prostatic disease is common in elderly male dogs, just as it is in their human counterparts The prostate gland is situated around the urethra just below the bladder. The gland is responsible for producing some of the secretions that make up the seminal fluid ejaculated by the dog during sexual intercourse. By far the most common disorder is an overgrowth of the gland due to the effect of male hormones, known as prostatic hyperplasia, followed by infections of the gland. Cancerous tumours and cysts of the prostate can also occur, but are far less common. Prostatic disorders can cause the passing of blood or pus in the urine and the enlarged prostate pushing upon the bowel or bladder can cause severe straining, usually to pass motions. This can in turn cause a perineal hernia to develop (*see* above). It is usually possible to detect an enlarged prostate gland by a rectal examination, but in some cases it is necessary to confirm the diagnosis by taking an X-ray.

Unlike humans, surgical removal of the enlarged prostate gland is not feasible, but prostatic hyperplasia can be cured by castration, either surgically or by giving anti-testosterone injections (this type of drug therapy is often used together with antibiotics in cases of prostatic infection). Medical treatment may be preferable in a very old and frail patient, but it will probably be necessary to give the injections regularly over an extended period and possibly for the rest of the dog's life. Female hormone tablets can also be given to produce a similar effect, but are more likely to produce side-effects. Surgical treatment of prostatic cysts is much more difficult, and the outlook for cases of prostatic cancer is very poor indeed.

PYOMETRA

In this condition the womb fills up with pus, which usually becomes infected. It is very common in elderly bitches, and is one very strong reason in favour of spaying bitches before they become old. Surgery is almost always necessary, and the risks involved are far less for a young and healthy bitch than for an elderly one that is ill due to an enlarged and infected womb. Pyometra tends to occur in the weeks following a season, and in some cases there is a heavy discharge from the vulva and the diagnosis is obvious. In other cases the cervix at the base of the womb remains closed and pus builds up internally without any external sign. Affected bitches tend to drink more than normal, and may subsequently become incontinent when shut indoors. As the condition develops, they go off their food, become obviously unwell, and often start to vomit. The abdomen may be obviously enlarged. If left untreated, the bitch will eventually die either due to rupture of the womb and internal infection, or because of the toxic effects of poisons released from the pus upon the liver and kidneys.

The diagnosis of cases of 'closed pyometra' – that is infection without a vulval discharge – can be very difficult. A blood test may help to show if the white blood cells are reacting to an infection, and an X-ray or ultrasound scan may well show up the enlarged womb. In some cases the only way to confirm the diagnosis is by an exploratory operation.

Once the diagnosis has been confirmed, it is best to remove the womb without delay, as bitches with a pyometra can deteriorate rapidly. The operation is a major procedure in an elderly bitch, and will usually require a period of intravenous fluid therapy and hospitalisation. Antibiotics alone do not generally cure the condition, although they are used as an adjunct to treatment. Some cases of successful treatment of the condition with a drug known as prostaglandin have been reported, although this drug has not been licensed for use in the dog and severe side effects are possible. It is probably best reserved as a last resort in cases where surgery has been ruled out for one reason or another.

RHINITIS

Rhinitis is an inflammation of the nasal passages and is often combined with sinusitis, an inflammation in the chambers within the bones of the skull that connect into the nasal passages. It can be caused by an infection within the nose, either bacterial, viral, or with a fungus called *Aspergillus fumigatus*, although this fungus is more often found in younger dogs, as are allergies. Foreign bodies such as grass seeds frequently enter the nose and cause a reaction. Unfortunately, tumours within the nasal cavity are also common in older dogs, and are usually cancerous.

Signs of rhinitis include sneezing, a nasal discharge, and sometimes a swelling on the outside of the nose. The dog may show signs of discomfort by pawing at its nose or pressing its head into the corner of a wall. Antibiotics will often be used as a first line of treatment, but if the dog does not respond it may be necessary to administer an anaesthetic and X-ray the nose. In larger dogs, it may also be possible to look up into the nose from the nostril with a fine fibre-optic examination light, and a blood test may help with the diagnosis of fungal infections.

Infections will usually respond to the appropriate antibiotic treatment, although if the infection is very well established, the damage to the lining of the nose may be so severe that only long-term control is possible. The surgical removal of foreign bodies and non-cancerous growths is feasible, although it does involve major surgery cutting into the bones of the skull. With cancerous tumours, the outlook is obviously very poor, although it is sometimes possible to give the dog a useful lease of life by treating it with antibiotics and anti-inflammatory drugs. It is also possible to give drugs to soften the mucus in the nose to dogs suffering from rhinitis, although one of the best palliative treatments is to take the dog into the bathroom with you when you have a bath, and let it get a good inhalation of steam.

SENILITY

We all know what senility means when applied to humans, and there is every evidence to suggest that dogs can also suffer from a progressive deterioration of their mental faculties as they age. This is often coupled with a dulling of the senses, such as hearing and sight, resulting in a reduced awareness of the surroundings, and often stumbling, incontinence and general confusion. This is much more difficult to measure in a dog than in a human, but owners that have grown used to the normal behaviour patterns of their dog over the years are generally very sensitive to changes.

There is obviously no magical cure for old age, but there are things that can be done to help a dog in this condition. A general physical examination and a blood test to highlight any specific underlying problems that can be treated should be carried out and those problems treated when possible. An easily digested diet with extra vitamins but no excesses of protein or minerals such as phosphorus can help to improve the dog's general state of health. There is now a relatively new drug on the market called propentofylline (marketed as Vivitonin) which acts by increasing the energy supply to muscle and nervous tissue, and in some dogs has a very marked effect in improving their level of alertness and physical activity, and sometimes even controlling more severe problems such as incontinence. Of course, there is a limit to what drug treatment can achieve, and if a dog is unable to live a reasonably normal lifestyle, then euthanasia may be the kindest option.

SKIN DISEASE

Skin disease is very common throughout the life span of the dog, with the two main causes being parasitic infestations and allergies. Older dogs may continue to be troubled with these problems, but as the dog gets older the skin undergoes changes that can spark off other troubles. As outlined in chapter 2, the skin tends to become less elastic and thin with age, and the production of the natural oils to protect the coat decreases. This can lead to a dry and scaly coat, that can sometimes be helped by giving an extra fatty acid supplement to the diet such as fish oil.

Some of the hormonal imbalances that occur in elderly dogs may also have an effect upon the skin, usually causing alopecia (baldness), particularly over the flanks. These hormonal problems include Cushing's Disease, hypothyroidism and testicular tumours.

Warts and cysts within the skin affect many elderly dogs, warts grow out of the skin and have an obvious 'neck' at their attachment, whereas cysts develop in or just under the skin, are roughly spherical in shape and are filled with fluid or semi-fluidal material. The most common form is the pilosebaceous cyst, which develops from the glands which produce the sebaceous secretion on the hairs, and these cysts tend to fill up with a toothpaste-like fatty substance. Neither warts nor skin cysts are a serious health risk, although warts sometimes become infected or damaged and then bleed, and cysts sometimes burst open and allow infection to enter. In these circumstances they may well need treating with antibiotics and possibly surgical removal. It is vital to distinguish these harmless growths from cancerous tumours, and if you are in any doubt at all, it is always best to have them checked. Even the experienced eye of a veterinary surgeon cannot always be certain that a growth is harmless, and if there is any doubt, it is best to have it removed and examined under the microscope by a pathologist to find out.

STROKES

Dogs do not suffer from atherosclerosis (clogging up of the arteries with fatty deposits) in the same way as humans, and so they do not suffer exactly the same condition as human strokes. However, they do quite commonly suffer from what are more correctly termed 'cerebrovascular accidents', where the blood supply to part of the brain is suddenly cut off. This is similar to a human stroke. An affected dog will lose its sense of balance, often becoming unable to stand, and will frequently show a head tilt to one side, or even a twisting of the head, neck and upper body in one direction. The eyes can usually be seen to flicker from side to side, a condition known as nystagmus, caused by damage to the part of the brain that controls the sense of balance and co-ordination.

It is very distressing for owners to see their pet afflicted by this condition, but recovery to a normal quality of life is possible in many cases. Drugs to increase the blood supply to the brain and reduce inflammation may help with the recovery, but as with human stroke victims, time is the greatest healer. Careful nursing is necessary to help the dog through the initial difficult period, and to give enough time to see if a recovery is going to occur. Eating and drinking may be difficult, and the dog might be unable to get outdoors to relieve himself. Signs of an improvement will normally be seen within 48 hours, and euthanasia should be considered if this is not occurring. Some dogs are left with a permanent head tilt to one side, giving them a somewhat quizzical look, but not generally interfering with their ability to live a normal lifestyle.

TUMOURS

Last alphabetically among the older dog problems, but by no means least, tumours become increasingly common with age, although when they develop in older animals they tend to grow more slowly than if they do occur earlier on in life. They can broadly be divided into benign tumours, which do not spread to other parts of the body and are not generally life-threatening, and malignant tumours, or cancers. A cancerous tumour will usually grow more quickly than a benign one, will invade the surrounding tissues, will often ulcerate if it is close to the surface of the skin and will tend to travel in the lymph or blood vessels to other parts of the body. The most common sites for these secondary tumours is in the lung and the liver, but they can occur in any position. The demarcation between cancerous and benign tumours is not clear-cut, and some tumours can vary in their degree of malignancy from one case to another. Others, such as some types of bone tumour, are always highly malignant and always spread to other parts of the body by the time a diagnosis has been reached.

There are many different types of tumour and they can develop in any tissue within the body. A very common benign growth in older dogs is the lipoma, which can be felt as a separate, round, soft lump between the skin and the muscle tissue below. Lipomas are made up of fatty tissue, and are more common in obese dogs. They sometimes cause problems because of their sheer size and have to be surgically removed. Another common growth in older dogs is a spleen tumour. These are also usually benign. Diagnosis is more difficult, because they develop within the abdomen and do not become obvious until they are very large. Problems can be caused by the pressure they exert on other organs such as the stomach, or because they are fragile and can easily bleed internally if damaged. Removal of the spleen is quite a major operation, but fortunately dogs can manage perfectly well without it, and can live for several years after such an operation.

Tumours of the white blood cells, known as leukaemia, when the cells in the blood are affected, and lymphosarcoma, when it affects the white cells in the lymph nodes, are particularly prevalent in middle-age, but can also affect older dogs. Leukaemia tends to cause general lethargy and loss of condition, and sometimes the lymph nodes themselves are obviously enlarged and can be felt by your vet. Diagnosis of leukaemia can be carried out with a blood test, but a surgical biopsy of an affected node is usually necessary in the case of lymphosarcoma.

Tumours of the reproductive organs can be prevented by early neutering, which is particularly important in the case of breast cancer, as it is extremely common in entire bitches, often necessitating major surgery. Male dogs sometimes get tumours of the testicle. These are often benign but produce feminising hormones that cause strange signs such as nipple development and hair loss.

The first question that the owner of a dog that is diagnosed as suffering from cancer usually asks, often somewhat guiltily, is 'why did it happen?'. Although we know that breast cancer in bitches and anal adenomas (see earlier) around the anus of male dogs are stimulated by the presence of sex hormones, we do not generally know what causes a tumour to develop. The body is continually producing cells that are potentially cancerous, and the defence mechanisms of the body destroy them before they have a chance to cause any problems. We know of certain carcinogens that encourage tumours to get a hold, such as cigarette smoking in humans, but we do not really understand what triggering factors are important in the dog.

Leukaemia and lymphosarcoma can often be treated quite successfully by chemotherapy, the use of drugs to control the cancer. Very large doses are used in humans in the hope of effecting a complete cure, but in dogs we generally aim to use lower doses of a combination of chemotherapeutic drugs in order to minimise any side effects. In this way we do not cure the problem, but can often give a dog a very useful lease of life for two years or more.

A major form of treatment for tumours is surgical excision – removing an area of apparently normal tissue from around the growth whenever possible to reduce the likelihood of re-growth. Sometimes a biopsy will be carried out first to identify the type of tumour involved and assess the best therapeutic approach and likely prognosis. In some parts of the country it is possible to obtain radiotherapy treatment, often used as a backup after surgical excision to mop up any remaining cancer cells, but sometimes on its own. Certain types of tumour are more responsive to radiotherapy than others, and the treatment always has to be carried out under anaesthetic.

There are many factors to be weighed up in deciding how to treat tumours, and indeed, whether treatment is in the best interests of the animal and its owner. Cost is one of those factors, and it is certainly one area where pet insurance comes into its own to cover the cost of veterinary fees. Sometimes, particularly in a very elderly pet, a decision may be made to withold any invasive treatment and put the dog to sleep once its quality of life begins to suffer.

6. Food for health

The basic principles of feeding for health earlier on in life have been dealt with in chapter 3, and the same basic principles apply through into old age. However, as a dog gets older his nutritional demands may well change:

CALORIES The metabolic rate and level of physical activity slows down with age, so calorific requirements gradually reduce. Older dogs are unable to use the food that they eat as efficiently as a younger dog, so feeding the same amount of food will result in a gradual increase in weight. As we have already seen, this can exacerbate a whole range of problems that are common in elderly dogs, such as arthritis and certain types of tumour.

PROTEIN There is no evidence that a healthy elderly dog has any different biological need for protein than a younger one, or that reduced protein levels will help to prevent kidney problems from developing. Having said this, kidney disease is extremely common in older dogs, and clinical signs only develop once the condition is quite advanced. There is a rational argument in favour of feeding older dogs a diet with moderately restricted levels of easily digestible protein to put less strain upon the kidneys of dogs that are beginning to develop problems (see below for more information about the role of protein levels in the diet in dogs clinically affected with kidney problems).

FAT Fat is very high in energy, so high levels in the diet will contribute towards obesity. Older dogs that are thin due to a fussy appetite may therefore benefit from increased levels of fat in the diet, which also improves the palatability of the diet. Many older dogs do not absorb essential fatty acids from the diet as efficiently as they used to, leading to a dry skin, poor coat quality and hair loss. Supplementation with vegetable oil may help, or better still, the addition of capsules of evening primrose oil, which is high in an essential fatty acid called gamma linolenic acid (GLA) has a particularly beneficial effect.

FIBRE Moderately increased levels of fibre in the diet of an elderly dog will help to reduce problems of constipation and reduce the calorific concentration of the food, so that the dog will feel satiated after feeding without putting on excess weight.

VITAMINS There is a common misconception that if vitamins are good, more vitamins must be better. Care must be taken not to over-supplement the diet, as an excess of some vitamins, such as A and E, can be harmful. A healthy elderly dog eating a balanced diet does not need an extra supplementation, but a dog that is not eating well in its old age may well not be taking in enough vitamins, and will usually benefit from the addition of a balanced supplement to the diet, particularly if the dog is being fed on a fresh meat diet rather than one that is pre-prepared.

MINERALS The need of a healthy elderly dog is very much the same as that earlier in life, but reduced levels of phosphorus and salt may be advisable in dogs suffering from kidney and heart disease respectively (see below). Just as with kidney disease, ensuring that excessive amounts of these minerals are not fed will prevent the diet from exacerbating the problem in dogs that are developing early signs of one of these problems.

In summary, a healthy elderly dog should ideally be fed on a diet that has:

- Moderately restricted levels of high quality protein
- Moderate levels of fat, possibly supplemented with an essential fatty acid additive
- Mildly increased levels of fibre
- Moderately restricted levels of phosphorus and salt.

Complete diets are now commercially available to provide this ideal balance for an elderly dog, and are the easiest way to ensure that the ideal balance of nutrients are being fed for that stage in your dog's life. It is possible to produce a similar diet by feeding good quality fresh meat plus mixer, with some added wheat bran to increase the fibre levels and a balanced mineral and vitamin supplement with a little extra corn oil. Only about one third of the total bulk should be fed as meat. There are no hard and fast rules regarding the quantity that should be fed to a particular dog, and the best way to judge this is by weighing the dog regularly to ensure its weight is stable.

Losing weight?

Although obesity can often be a problem in old age, many older dogs are often more finicky with the foods that they will eat, choosing to eat little and often, and may have problems with weight loss, particularly if they are suffering from some underlying clinical condition. Many older dogs have rather fewer teeth than in their younger days, and will therefore find it difficult to eat hard food, or food that requires a lot of tearing and chewing, such as lumps of raw meat, (of course, if a dog has a sore mouth, it should receive veterinary attention – *see* dental disease in chapter 5). A veterinary health check is strongly advisable for an elderly dog that is eating as much as it wants yet is losing weight.There are several things you can do to tempt your dog to eat:-

- Mix in small amounts of a highly palatable food such as chicken.
- Hand feed the food.
- Prepare the food in small amounts – small cans are better than large ones if possible, as the act of opening a can seems to excite the tastebuds of many dogs.
- Adding some sugar may aid palatability, as will some strong-smelling herbs, such as garlic.
- Increase the amount of fat in the diet.

SPECIAL DIETS FOR SPECIAL PROBLEMS

Dietary management is an important part in the control of many disease problems, and many older dogs will have special feeding requirements relating to a specific problem. Commercially produced diets are now available from veterinary surgeries for many of these conditions and if your dog accepts them, they are designed to provide the ideal balance of nutrients to control that particular problem, and still provide all the normal maintainance requirements of the dog. Any change of diet should be gradual, mixing the new food in increasing proportions over several days, or stomach upsets could result. The principles of dietary management for various diseases are listed below, but if you prefer to prepare something haute cuisine for your dog, (or if your dog has you so well trained that it will accept nothing less!), a recipe section is included at the end of this chapter.

Kidney disease

Many of the signs caused by kidney disease result from an accumulation of waste products produced by the breakdown of protein in the body, combined with a loss of calcium and a build-up of phosphorus, which in turn damages the kidneys further. A change in diet is one of the most useful measures that can be taken to improve condition and slow down further deterioration, because once kidney tissue is scarred, it cannot regenerate. The sooner that the diet is changed, the better, as once the dog becomes unwell and more picky with food, the less chance there is of getting him to accept the new diet.

A diet that has restricted levels of protein, phosphorus and salt, with extra B vitamins, needs to be fed. The degree of protein restriction depends on the severity of the disease, measured by monitoring blood urea levels. Urea is one of the poisonous substances produced in the body by the breakdown of protein, and if the level is very high, then an ultra-low protein diet must be fed, providing just enough protein to maintain the body musculature, but ensuring that the energy requirements of the dog are met from other sources such as fat and carbohydrate. The protein also needs to be of a very high quality so that the dog does not have to break down more than it needs to provide its requirements. In milder cases of renal disease, the level of protein in the diet can be correspondingly higher.

If you are feeding a home-made low-protein diet, your vet will advise you on the amount of protein that is suitable for your particular dog, but it should be fed in the form of fresh meat or eggs, and not offal. The quality of the protein in a normal canned or dry dog food is fine for a healthy dog, but is not sufficiently high for a dog with kidney disease. Dogs with kidney disease often have a fussy appetite, and the diet can be supplemented with starchy foods or fatty foods, such as sweet biscuits, bread and butter, pasta or potatoes, but extra protein must not be given. A plentiful supply of water must be available at all times, as the dog will almost certainly be drinking more than usual.

Several manufacturers make pre-prepared diets for dogs with kidney disease, and in this way you can be certain that you are giving the ideal balance of nutrients to control the problem. These foods come canned or in dry form, and it is worth trying both with fussy dogs, as some will refuse one but enthusiastically tuck into the other. You can aid the transition to the new diet by mixing in some of your dog's favourite foods, but should aim to feed just the prescribed diet.

Heart disease

This is common in elderly dogs, and particularly in some breeds such as the Cavalier King Charles Spaniels and Miniature Poodles, that are prone to a degeneration of the heart valves as they age. The decreased efficiency of the heart pump causes a build-up of fluid in the chest and abdomen, and an accumulation of sodium. Feeding a low-salt diet is therefore an essential part in the control of this problem, and should be instituted as soon as a heart problem is diagnosed. Commercially prepared diets for dogs with heart disease are available, but it is quite easy to cook a diet of fresh meat and rice or pasta that will have a low salt content. Dogs find salt very palatable, and most ordinary dog foods and mixers contain quite high levels of salt. Bread, processed meats and many forms of offal are also high in salt and should be avoided. It is important that a dog with heart disease is not overweight, as this will put an extra strain on the heart.

Liver disease

The liver is vital as a factory for the processing of many of the nutrients that the body needs, and liver problems usually result in a poor appetite and severe digestive problems. The diet needs to be highly palatable and easily digestible, with moderately restricted levels of high quality protein, and it should be fed little and often. Extra vitamins will compensate for those not being processed properly by the liver and aid its recovery, and an amino acid called methionine has a specific action in helping the liver to function. There are no diets specifically designed for dogs with liver disease at the present time, but the needs can be met by feeding the same diet that would be used for mild cases of kidney disease.

Obesity

Dogs are naturally greedy creatures, because in the wild they have to gorge themselves on as much food as possible, as quickly as they can, before their catch is eaten by other members of the pack. Given an ad lib supply of food, most dogs will become overweight, and some breeds, such as Labradors and Beagles, are particularly prone to obesity. Increasing the fibre content of the food to make the dog feel that its stomach is full will encourage the dog to take in less calories. Again, proprietary low-calorie dog foods are now available, although a similar effect can be achieved by adding some wheat bran to the food. Regular weighing is very useful to pick up fluctuations in body weight.

Constipation

This is another problem that will usually respond to a high fibre diet to soften the motions. Bones should not be fed, as dogs will often swallow splinters that can harden the motions, or cause even more serious damage. A laxative, such as liquid paraffin, can be used to lubricate the passage of the motions, but repeated use can lead to a deficiency of the fat-soluble vitamins, such as vitamin A. Faecal modifiers that absorb moisture and soften the motions are available from vets, and are the best way of maintaining the consistency of the faeces in the long term.

Diabetes

Diabetics need a very stable diet so that insulin requirements do not fluctuate too much, and this is best achieved by feeding a veterinary prescription diet designed for the purpose. Diabetics used to be fed on very low carbohydrate diets, but recent work has shown that it is not the quantity, but the type of carbohydrate that matters. The ideal diet should be low in fat, contain a moderate amount of good quality protein, and high levels of what are known as complex carbohydrates, such as maize and rice starch. Sugary snacks must be avoided at all costs. High levels of fibre help to slow down the absorption of glucose from the bowel, which makes it easier for the diabetic to cope, and will also help to avoid obesity, which is common in diabetics.

Diarrhoea and/or vomiting

Dogs with a digestive upset are generally best starved for 24 hours, and then put onto a light diet that is low in fat and fibre. White meat, or white fish with a little carbohydrate, such as boiled rice, is best, and should be fed little and often. No attempt should be made to feed an ordinary diet until the problem has thoroughly cleared, and then the change should be made gradually over a few days. Some dogs seem unable to digest canned foods and have to be kept on a fresh meat diet, or a special prescription diet designed for dogs with chronic digestive problems.

Post-surgical diet

Follow the directions given by your veterinary surgeon closely in the immediate post-operative period. In some cases, dogs may be able to have a light meal in the evening after having been given an anaesthetic, but in other cases, particularly after surgery on the bowel, it may be necessary to withold food for a period. The same principles of feeding outlined above for an elderly dog with a fussy appetite may also be applied to nursing a dog after an operation. Sometimes it may be necessary to force-feed a liquid food with a syringe by holding the head of the dog back and gently dribbling the food into the mouth, but great care must be taken to give the food slowly so that it is not inhaled into the lungs, as this can start up a pneumonia and cause a lot more harm than good. Special liquid dog foods are available for this purpose. Dogs that are unwilling or unable to eat for an extended period can be hospitalised and fed with either a pharyngostomy tube, which is implanted under a light anaesthetic to enter the gullet through a skin incision in the side of the neck and into the stomach, or a nasogastric tube, which is a very fine tube that is passed down one nostril and down into the stomach. Both these means of feeding are tolerated suprisingly well by most dogs.

7. Behaviour at home

Our dogs' behaviour changes as they grow older. Many of the changes are predictable because they are very similar to those that we experience – for example, changing activity cycles and greater demands for sleep in old age. They may reflect similar underlying emotional changes too, such as greater feelings of insecurity. Different things are important to dogs at different stages of life. While we all love the innocent playfulness of the exploring young puppy and readily forgive nuisances such as chewed slippers and occasional puddles on the floor, once the dog enters adolescence we become far less forgiving. We suspect that the dog is being deliberately disobedient or testing his will against ours.

In many cases, he is, because that is what is what he is supposed to do at this stage. All adolescents, human and canine, do it, and it's no surprise that most of the cases referred to members of the Association of Pet Behaviour Counsellors (APBC) concern adolescent dogs, particularly the more competitive males, and that most people who reject their dogs and have them euthanased, take them to an animal rescue shelter or rehome them, do so before the dog could be regarded as socially mature. If the dog can survive its own puberty and integrate well into its human pack, then there's a good chance that it will survive to enjoy its old age, loved and treated with the same patience and level of discipline as one would a child and itself adopting a low-ranking, compliant and largely non-challenging attitude towards its human packmate companions.

As man and dog learn to adapt, respect and take pleasure in each other, and learn to cope with each other's idiosyncrasies, the slow onset of age and its effects on the physical and mental abilities of the dog are gradually accommodated as they affect the relationship. By the time the dog's old age is clearly signalled by a declining demand for social activity, fewer walks and greater demand for sleep, most owners will have developed a loving respect for their old trooper, even if the dog has become more difficult to care for physically and perhaps a little truculent. There's something about the calm, experienced, yet sometimes intransigent, disposition of old dogs that usually demands respect, even if some aspects of their reactive behaviour, such as grumbling, would not be so well tolerated in a younger dog.

CHANGES IN CHARACTER

While some dogs have a more peaceful attitude to life, others manage to maintain a youthful exuberance that belies their age. Some, of course, can become rather crotchety and prefer to be left undisturbed. As these types can often be the most memorable and bias one's impressions of how older dogs behave, we asked owners if their dog's character had changed as it aged and if so, how.

The majority of owners wrote that their dog had become more of a pleasure to live with. Only 9 per cent reported that it was now less enjoyable and 11 per cent that their pleasure rating had not changed. But, the level of dissatisfaction did grow with the dog's advancing years once past 13 years of age, and 33 per cent of owners described their dog as being less enjoyable to own by the time he or she reached the grand age of 15 years.

A mellow old age

Sixty-three owners summed up the positive changes in their dog's character as being more affectionate or loving. This would clearly make owners more willing to cope with any physical limitations or demands made on them by their old dog. Many other older dogs (34) were reported as being more docile, quiet, placid, calm, relaxed, dignified, confident and tolerant in old age.

Some owners were pleased to report that their dogs were far less hyperactive, 'silly' or 'naughty' in their old age, perhaps because they were more settled and less worried about stirring up their human pack for a little action or testing their position in the pack through a little contrived defiance. One male dog was less likely to try and escape to go roaming in search of the lady dogs. This is a typical testosterone-inspired pastime of many a male with a glint in his eye. In old age, it's not so much that the motivation disappears even if hormone output does decline a little, but the flesh won't scale the fence or dart so quickly through a chink of light in the gate. Perhaps it saves disappointment, because even if he does get out and strike lucky, his back legs may not be able to stand the weight of his amorous intent any more, and frustration of that sort feels bad at any age!

One improved old dog was very nicely described as 'mellow', a word which perhaps reflects how we would all like to view life in our our old age . . . settled, unrufflable and with an air of self-confidence that perhaps only many years of life and a contented home can bring.

Increasing dependence

On the other hand, some dogs are clearly aware of their declining abilities to look after themselves and become more anxious and dependent on their owners in old age. Simply being prepared to offer more time can keep an older dog happy. Some dogs became more demanding, fussy, dependent and needed to be touched a lot, which clearly underlines the need to make more time available to look after the older dog when he is awake. Some dogs in our survey had become more anxious, clinging to owners and following them around the house. For owners used to being an emotional prop for their dog (many owners enjoy the parental role that this type of relationship confers upon them), the extra dependency of their dog in old age will enhance their appreciation of their dog. For others, by whom greater emotional dependency is seen as a tie, the demands of keeping their older dog content in his old age through constant company can cause rejection at the very time when the dog needs their support most.

That said, of course, dogs are expert social manipulators and, in the early stages of old age, may simply be giving the impression of vulnerability rather than face minor threats and challenges that they dealt with well when younger. When treating nervous or phobic dogs of any age, it's important to distinguish between learned helplessness and incompetence and genuine sensitivity and fear. Many owners are blissfully unaware that their apparently helpless, socially incompetent dog is, in fact, a highly confident character away from their side. A little relationship restructuring with owners initiating more of the social contact with their dog and being rather less responsive to its demands for attention, even in old age, can often remedy the situation and keep the dog in a more confident frame of mind and continuing to face up to life's little challenges without constant back up.

Mr Grumpy

But while the majority of dogs seem to improve in character with age either passively or actively and thus become even more enjoyable for their owners, some became more stubborn, intolerant, grumpy, irritable, spiteful or snappy. One owner described that, as her old dog's eyesight had failed, he had become more macho towards everything and everybody. But, assuming that all social aggression is in fact born out of fear and the need to protect oneself, in all cases the older dog must have been approached by the owner before he demonstrated these less desirable qualities. Doubtless many of those approaches were either reasonable: 'Come on Bonzo, time to get up to take a trip to the garden',' or 'Let's have a look at those ears and gums of yours,' or unavoidable, 'I was only walking past your bed, Bonzo!.' But the dog perceived a threat to his position and security and, aware of being less able in old age to avoid or deflect the challenge, he may have seen no other option but to react with a counter-threat of a growl or snap. In truth, he only wanted to be left alone, and several owners reported that their dog did indeed like to be left alone far more than in earlier times. Perhaps many of those described as 'aggressive' wouldn't be so grumpy or snappy if they were left to their own devices more. Sometimes, we can be too caring in the wrong way in trying to force comfort and attention on our pets and it's no surprise that they don't always want it!

By and large, the circumstances under which the irritability of old age rears its ugly head can at least be predicted and managed, and thus not detract from the other benefits of owning an older dog that is quiet and less demanding. Unless, of course, there is some on-going medical complaint that requires frequent close attention or treatment. In such cases, it's always best never to attempt such close handling in the dog's bed or resting areas, but to do so outdoors where he will be less defensive and more compliant. If there's still trouble, then for non-oral examinations, either muzzle and restrain him first to speed the entire process or, best of all, let the vet do it!

Barking

While many dogs might be expected to abdicate the role of protecting their home territory as they get older, some dogs become more insistent on protecting their owners in old age. Again, a greater level of barking and defence behaviour could be expected in some dogs in the same way as loss of temper occurs more quickly in some older people when socially challenged. It's all part of the same self-defence strategy of course, and dogs that have always been active and successful in barking at the door (they don't know that the departing postman was leaving to deliver the post next door and not just retreating from the bark) will sometimes accentuate their reactions when older. The louder the noise and the bigger the display, the less likely they are to suffer strangers on their ever more vital home base, or approaches and investigations that might expose their increased physical vulnerability in old age. Though annoying for owners and their neighbours, it's usually a successful policy for the dog and only declines when his hearing starts to deteriorate and he can't hear the footsteps on the drive or the ring at the door!

Exercise

One of the most commonly noted physical signs of old age is a stiffening of legs or back either on a walk or after returning home. One would expect most dogs to become more reluctant to engage in physical activity as they age and perhaps alter their activity patterns becoming more willing to exchange a cuddle and rub and short romp at home for long periods of exercise. Some respondents to the survey reported that their dogs did not seem to enjoy exercise as much as in their youth but the canine spirit is still willing to walk even if sometimes the oldest flesh is a bit weak and takes a while to recover afterwards. See chapter 9 for advice on exercise changes.

If your older dog isn't so bothered nowadays about maintaining canine rights of access to a regularly used walking area and is happy to leave the leg lifting, flirtation and minor social confrontations to younger and more competitive locals, and if he long ago gave up being interested in chasing squirrels, then reduced frequency or length of outdoor walks will not result in a great loss of quality of life for him, provided we play with him at home. It all depends on the individual dog of course, but the important thing to remember is that whether physical exercise and stimulation away from home is reduced or structured in the dog's old age because he chooses to do less, or he is physically unable to enjoy so much or because he needs a little protection from his own own enthusiasm, we owners must make the effort to offer compensatory activity and stimulation at home and in the garden as activity off base declines. See chapter 9 for some play suggestions.

Sleep

Most people sleep more as they get older, until some variable point in late middle age when they may not only sleep far less but also in a very different cycle. It is by no means uncommon for elderly people only to need four or five hours sleep per day and to take much of this in short spells, particularly in the afternoon, not only finding sleep difficult at night but also being unable to concentrate on other activities if they are awake then. Similar disruptions can occur to the sleep patterns of dogs as they age, particularly in terms of taking more sleep in frequent dozes during the day. One owner reported how her dog enjoys 'a very deep sleep in the evening' and most described how their older dog tended to sleep especially after walks or play at home and after meals. Most older dogs in the survey seemed to enjoy a good night's sleep however much they slept during the day and few older dogs seem to suffer from any form of insomnia. One owner, however, did complain of 'broken nights as he cries to be let out', but this was probably due to the dog waking because he needed to relieve himself.

In the *Dogs Today* survey, one respondent wrote 'he takes himself off to bed more often now' and most owners mentioned that their dogs slept more as they aged. Eighty per cent reported that their dog slept more after the age of 11 and 90 per cent by the age of 15 years and it is clear from the survey that there is a linear rise in the percentage of dogs sleeping more with every year after the age of 7.

Many dogs take themselves off to bed more often or fall asleep wherever they settle after exercise. 'He sleeps unless there is food around or the prospect of a walk,' wrote one lady, while another less committed slumberer 'sleeps unless there is something more interesting going on' which sounds like a reasonable attitude to adopt.

However, because older dogs seem to become more and more attached to their owners as they age, many dogs in the survey only felt secure enough to sleep when their owners sat down or the dog felt that they would stay in one place for a long enough time for them to relax.

'Sleeps wherever I am' was a common comment in the survey, and for this reason, many owners provided their older dogs with several beds in different rooms around the house. It would be wise for owners of attached older dogs to bear their dog's dilemma in mind and be aware that their dog isn't just feeling insecure and wanting the protection of their company in old age. The dog, particularly after exercise or a long period awake, may be desperate to sleep and needs its owner to sit down for a while so that it can settle. After a few minutes, perhaps as long as it takes to enjoy a cup of tea and a short energy boosting rest for the owner, the dog is highly likely to be asleep and the owner can tiptoe away to get on without causing upset.

One dog enjoyed the security of being able to lie on the scent of his owners through provision of old unwashed tee shirts in his bed, a simple gesture of reassurance which can help dogs of all ages feel more comfortable, especially if they are left on their own.

Of all respondents to the survey, only one or two said that they did not do anything in particular to make their dogs more comfortable in old age, perhaps because they already had provided super-comfortable facilities. But most owners were well aware of the need for extra comfort, warmth and support in the dog's bed to ease the pressure on the elderly resting body. A wide range of methods were cited of how owners had tried to help their old canines feel comfortable and secure while sleeping, including 'has been given the bed in the spare bedroom' and 'have moved over in my double bed to give him more room' to doggy beanbags, raised dog beds to keep out of draughts, sheepskins, frequently refilled hot water bottles, heat pads, goosedown duvets, extra blankets or rugs, mattresses, cushions and, in one case, even to offering herbal cushions to add warmth, softness and a touch of relaxing aromatherapy. One 12-year-old Collie had a 'double duvet folded with Vetbed (a synthetic sheepskin-like bedding) on top and a blanket underneath'! Another had a beanbag, a chair, a dog bed and a basket by the radiator.

Many owners kept the heating on all night or ensured their dog's bed was near the radiator or fire for warmth but, because of their attachment to their owners, many old dogs had, after many years of sleeping in the kitchen or utility room, finally managed to be discharged from guard duty and now slept in their owner's bedroom or even on the bed at night. One person described how her dog waited now to be lifted on to her bed in order to rest, while another had even removed the legs from their bed so that the dog could climb up with less trouble. Others had bought settees, mattresses or armchairs for their old pets and placed them in a warm quiet corner or installed them in their own bedrooms.

Senses and communication with old dogs

A dog's behaviour will alter as his senses change and we must be aware of these changes. See chapter 9 for tips and suggestions in communicating with dogs with failing eyesight and hearing.

SEPARATION ANXIETIES IN OLD AGE

Dogs are by nature, pack animals and rely on company for their own self confidence. Most dogs kept as pets will have to be alone at some point in their lives, most on a regular basis as we need to leave them to go to work, quite apart from wanting to enjoy a social life. Most puppies learn to cope with solitude after a few early experiences and though they may chew, whine or bark in response to their anxiety, they soon come to accept that being alone on occasion is part of life.

For some adult dogs, especially those not accustomed to being left alone when young, the experience is frightening and they suffer from a condition known as separation anxiety. The most common sign of this is displacement activity: destruction of household property, often accompanied by hyperactivity as the dog rushes round the house pausing only to chew at something; involuntary house soiling in otherwise house trained dogs; and barking and howling, which often causes problems with the neighbours. Some sufferers also try to escape the home and dig frantically at exit doors or nearby walls, often injuring their paws and mouths in the process. More rarely encountered and usually more difficult to treat are self-mutilation/hair pulling behaviours. Typically the dog becomes anxious as the owners leave the house, but may even be winding himself up as he recognises the signs of their imminent departure such as locking the back door, closing the windows, reaching for the car keys etc. Introverted canine characters tend to be whiners or self-mutilators when suffering from separation anxiety, while extroverts tend to attempt escape or are destructive or bark and howl maniacally when left. But sensitivity to such challenges does usually fall in adulthood and most adult dogs can be happily left at home alone, or perhaps in the secure and protected comfort of the car, without becoming so anxious. But for a few, such problems, long ago overcome, return in old age as their self-confidence falls and their dependence on their packmates increases.

In the *Dogs Today* survey, owners were asked about their dog's ability to be left alone. Most owners of course, had dogs that, perhaps after some initial difficulties with them as puppies, were quite able to be left and continued to be so in old age. Only about 10 per cent (52) reported that their dog's abilities in this respect had changed at all and, of these, 36 dogs had become worse in old age. But up to the age of 15, dogs were just as likely to be more relaxed about being left as to show signs of separation anxiety. Problems only became much more likely with very old dogs of 16 years or more, when senses were usually failing and perceptions of security away from the protection of packmates were probably at their lowest. Sixteen dogs who had shown growing signs of separation anxiety in adulthood had improved up to this point, probably because they had become generally calmer in old age and, because they slept more, found themselves waking up alone from time to time and so desensitized themselves to solitude.

The risk of problems

The risk of separation anxiety problems developing or returning in older dogs is undoubtedly greater in those who seem to need their owners around more. The survey owners who reported that their dog needed lots of human company for reassurance would be most at risk from the damage that sufferers of separation anxiety can cause in their panic. Special care should be taken to recognise and treat these problems early on, before the dog comes to depend on the the owner's physical presence round the clock for emotional security. For while the damage inflicted by an anxious dog may be tolerable up to a point, what is usually of far greater concern is the high level of distress that dogs, especially older ones, experience during such anxiety attacks.

Fortunately, even with older dependent dogs, treatment is usually effective provided all members of the family are consistent in their application of now well tested therapies developed by pet behaviour therapists. Therapy is aimed at helping the dog learn to cope with his own company by defining his relations with his owners better. It aims to make him less dependent on their physical presence; establishing a secure resting place in the home for him to retreat to when alone (*see* indoor kennels, pp. 93) and leaving security bridges. Progress can sometimes be slow initially, but even older dogs who have spent virtually all their lives in human company usually respond to treatment in the end. Severe cases can be assisted by certain drugs, such as sedatives, prescribed by the veterinary surgeon but these are used as vehicles to assist the early stages of treatment and are withdrawn steadily as the dog's ability to cope improves. The use of drugs may not be advisable with older dogs or those on other medications, but vets will obviously be able to advise about this.

A typical five-stage treatment plan is shown below. This may need to be adjusted in consultation with a professional pet behaviour counsellor to suit the individual circumstances.

Treatment Plan for Separation Anxiety

1. Stop all punishment as this confuses the dog as to his relationship with you. Always be pleased to see the dog on your return after separation. (Go outside and scream or kick the wall if your dog has caused damage!)

2. Encourage and reward independence in the dog by decreasing your overall contact time when together at home. Ignore your dog's demands for attention, food, play etc and only offer contact under your initiation

3. Systematically desensitize your dog to your departure by varying the routines and rituals of departure. Practise steadily increasing periods of solitude for the dog when you are at home. Play with or exercise your dog and feed him, place him in a secure bed (i.e. indoor kennel) to rest and hopefully sleep and then ignore him for 15 minutes prior to leaving. Do not stop to say 'goodbye' as this heightens dependence at the most crucial time prior to separation.

4. Provide security bridges, such as radios or videos (i.e. 'Cool for Dogs' by Peter Neville) playing, smell of old clothes in bed, chews and toys. Offer a safe bed/resting area, ideally an indoor kennel, where the dog will feel protected and restricted from causing damage. The dog should be encouraged to use the kennel for all periods of rest and, once he views it as a den, the door can perhaps be left open without risk and he can resume his role as a guard.

5. Another dog or even a cat may help keep the dog relaxed when left, though choose the companion with care as the 'wrong' dog could learn from the patient and double the scale of the problem!

Routines are important

Maintaining or introducing routines of activities such as feeding, walking and grooming are important to keep life predictable, and thus secure, for an old dog. For dogs which have become used to the working routines of their owners, changes can in themselves be most unsettling and confusing. With their own activity patterns very firmly mimicking those of their family, disruption can cause otherwise confident dogs to develop separation anxiety and other neurotic behaviours if their routine is disturbed.

8. Dogs together

Dogs, as we all know are pack animals, or at least descended from one of the most successful social animals that can live in packs, the wolf. The key to the wolf's success has been its ability to communicate effectively with pack members and develop a social structure in larger groups if the opportunities arise. Wolves' highly advanced social skills enable them to co-operate with each other to improve the pack's ability to exploit local circumstances. This also improves each individual's chances of survival, so ensuring the successful reproduction of the species.

But not all wolves live in packs. In fact, more wolves live in pairs or small family groups than large packs. The deciding factors as to how large a group develops from a breeding pair will usually be the availability of food and shelter during the harshest times of year, the levels of competition for those resources and degree of persecution by the wolf's only natural enemy, man.

Different breeds, different behaviour

The wolf has passed on its great social adaptability and skills of communication to our modern dogs along with its enormous physical adaptability and ability to exploit a range of environments through adopting different lifestyles. But, in the course of selection and breeding by man, our 450 or so modern breeds of dog have come to vary from their ancestor not only in the broad range of types and sizes observed, but also in their social behaviour and desire and ability to communicate with other.

Some, such the Husky and perhaps the German Shepherd Dog, are as able as their ancestor to communicate their moods to each other through facial expressions, body postures and movement sequences and so define their relative social standing. They need to develop a hierarchy, or rather, two hierarchies, one for each sex, when living in groups of the same breed.

Others, such as Norfolk Terriers still seem well able to communicate with each other but do not develop such a defined hierarchical system to govern their social relations. Their behaviour seems to mimic that of juvenile wolves in a pack, rather than emulate the more competitive adults for whom a harmonious pack life can only proceed successfully according to the observation of social rules.

The behaviour of the older pet dog in the human pack, both towards the people and the other dogs that it shares its life with and towards those dogs that it encounters outside the group, is thus likely to be enormously variable. One would expect, for instance, that previously high-ranking dogs of socially conscious breeds, such as the German Shepherd Dog, are more likely to experience distress as they age, when living in groups of others of the same breed and sex, if they lose a previously high position in the pack.

Demotion of older members is not usually an option in a wolf pack. Once the top dog is ousted by a younger fitter individual of the same sex, as he must be to ensure the fitness of the pack, he will be expelled from the group and probably adopt a solitary life until he dies shortly afterwards. Maintained in the human den, an older dog, simply by virtue of his presence, may present an on-going challenge to his replacement, leading to harassment and victimization and perhaps injury.

Fortunately, bitches, especially when spayed, are usually far less sensitive about the social order and so such problems are rarely encountered even in family packs of the socially sensitive breeds. Even more fortunately, most breeds and cross-breeds seem to be far less bothered about their place in the social order than the Wolf, German Shepherd Dog or Husky. And even most individuals within these breeds are not so competitive that the ageing of any individual will automatically present a problem for the owners. In any case, owners are usually regarded by all their dogs as the ultimate top dogs and this has a naturally suppressing effect on any rank squabbles lower down in the dog section of the human pack, keeping them all in order.

The commonest problems

The most common problems relating to shifts in social order due to the ageing of high-ranking dogs are encountered when owners keep the same sex dog of different breeds. When the social sensitivity of, say, a previously low-ranking German Shepherd Dog, forces him to seek to take over from a previously naturally more dominant (perhaps through a combination of hormonal influences, toughness, intelligence and better communication skills) but less bothered-about-it aging Labrador, serious fights can occur. This is simply because the Labrador does not comprehend what is going on nor why status has become so important to the German Shepherd Dog that he is now seizing his opportunity for promotion. It can present a serious problem for the owner, particularly as the older dog may suffer quite badly in any fights. Previously friendly dogs may need to be separated permanently, or one rehomed for his own protection, and the whole situation can be very upsetting.

If, as most of us do, we have one dog, or a pair of opposite sexes, or several of the less socially aware types, ageing of any one dog is unlikely to cause any problems at all. But if the natural instincts for survival and the motivations to oust the weak from the pack inherited from the wild ancestor do rear their head in our domesticated wolves, the drives can be just as unshakeable and just as ruthless in their impact. It's always worth remembering that even the breeds of dog that have been most modified from the wolf by us in terms of shape, size, appearance and sensitivity to social position in a pack, such as the Cavalier King Charles Spaniel, still exhibit about 80 per cent of the behavioural repertoire of the wolf. So the wild side of our pet dogs is never far away, no matter how peaceful your pet looks by the fireside!

RELATIONSHIP IN OLD AGE

By the time a dog enters old age, his attitudes towards other dogs and unfamiliar people will be well known to his owners and any problems will have been ironed out or have become predictable, and the owners will know how to manage any unwanted excesses. But by then, any remaining desire to rule the world and protect his resources may have become less of a vital issue, even for many reactive males. In the *Dogs Today* survey, a dog's reaction to meeting other dogs outside the home was reported to have changed in 25 per cent of respondents with older dogs, a figure which rose to over 50 per cent in dogs aged 15 years and over. Thirty-six owners of dogs over 10 years of age reported that their dog had certainly become less aggressive, more timid or friendlier towards other dogs.

Timidity certainly implies a greater willingness to run away to avoid any potential for disagreement with a dog looking to prove a point. Though for 'friendly', one should perhaps substitute the more accurate description of 'appeasing', as this type of older dog may now be attempting to ensure his own safety through mild submission and ingratiation when approached by another fitter and perhaps more competitive individual. In days past, he might have stood firm and expected the stranger to back away but now he has had to adopt a different strategy of avoiding conflict.

Of course the survey sample may be rather biased because known nasty characters will still have been largely kept away from other dogs and any improvements will have gone unrecorded by their owners. We were, perhaps, also more likely to hear from owners whose dogs were perfectly sociable with other dogs and had, like most of our pet dogs, quite a strong urge to play with others – engaging in competition and trials of strength on occasion, perhaps, but of a far less hazardous nature than the full physical competition of a fight.

From the survey figures, twelve years of age seems to be the watershed when the desire to play with other dogs, competitively or just for fun, slows down or stops and owners report their dogs to be largely ignoring other dogs. Nineteen owners wrote to say that after this age, and whatever their dog's previous attitude towards other dogs, he or she usually now just ignored others and did not even want to sniff or exchange greetings. They had become happy to be left to just potter about and get on with their own business. Perhaps this would correspond to the time when, in a wild dog or wolf pack, the older dog would be seen as having nothing further to contribute to the strength of the pack and would be driven away or simply left behind.

The short-tempered dog

However, 20 owners said that their dog had become more aggressive, grumpy or defensive in attitude since he reached ten years of age. The often-quoted undesirable characteristic of some people and dogs alike in old age is grumpiness and intolerance of unwanted social contact, but this is usually forward strategy in trying to avoid risk of injury. If employed properly, it can be just as effective at protecting the older dog as running away or making appeasing gestures to other dogs whose approach is perceived as threatening.

But, for as long as it works, the old pet dog may use the 'reactive grumpy' attitude to cover for his failing physical condition and sensory awareness and to protect his social position, individual freedom of movement and choice of action. Lacking the desire or need any more to initiate any contact or competition with other unfamiliar dogs, he will then happily live out his days as a largely undisturbed solitary animal, safe in the knowledge that he doesn't have to compete fully with any policy for the keys to survival because his human pack at home will feed him and keep him warm! Any playfulness that he still has in him is most likely to occur with real packmates, human or canine, with whom stable relationships have developed and who can be relied on to respect his physical limitations and desire to stop when he's had enough . . . though it takes a grumpy growl on occasion to underline the point!

ACQUIRING A NEW PUPPY

Many owners take the advice offered by many vets, trainers and breeders to take on a puppy to perk up their older dog a little and to keep him active, competing, playful and as youthful as possible in his final years. And, though a few older dogs are doubtless driven to an early grave by the constant pesterings of a playful young pup, or driven into the background by an extra-bouncy or competitive young character, by and large acquiring a young companion has always been considered a good idea to keep an older dog enjoying life to the full.

No less than 55 per cent of respondents to the *Dogs Today* survey had taken on a puppy while they still had their existing dog, with the likelihood of doing so increasing with the age of the older dog. Doubtless some new pups were taken not so much to stimulate a very old and perhaps inactive dog into a new lease of life but, anticipating the imminent demise of the old trooper, to cushion the blow of the loss for the owners. The new puppy would help ensure that, after so long, there would still be a dog around the house to make it feel less empty afterwards and make them keep up the routines of feeding, walking and caring.

Positive reactions

Reactions from older dogs to their newcomers varied from love to hate: from 'curious' to 'ignored him completely' and from 'follows him everywhere and licks him all over at every opportunity' to 'became bloody minded and disobedient' – presumably an attempt to attract attention away from the new arrival and keep it firmly where it belonged! But, even where there was an initial unpleasant reaction, most introductions seemed to work out fine in the end and the two dogs became friends, to the particular benefit of the older dog. Over 100 replies were very positive, 43 saying their old dog mothered or loved the new one and 7 specifically stating that the arrival of a new puppy gave their oldie a brand new lease of life.

Most dogs are likely to enjoy the company of any new dog introduced into the pack because the dog is a social animal and new relationships will increase the quality of life and enhance feelings of personal security that result from being in a larger group with a more intricate social structure. In single dog households, of course, the arrival of another dog gives the resident the chance for social interaction and opportunity for play of the canine kind, when, despite a usually good relationship with his owners, there are always inevitably so many areas of miscommunication between them and types of social interaction which only dogs want to get involved with, like licking each others' ears!

Negative reactions

On the negative side in the survey, 23 owners reported that their existing older dog was wary, snappy and jealous of the newcomer at first. Most went on to report that the older dog came to accept the pup eventually, even if it ignored it at first and subsequently kept it under firm control, telling it off sometimes quite harshly when he or she had had enough of the pup leaping all over them or found the young upstart in their resting place. Other more 'middle-of-the-road' comments concerning the reactions of the older dog included 'puzzled but livelier' and 'dignified resignation'. Several mentioned that the older dog ignored the new one as an irrelevant non-competitive child until it was six months to a year old and started to mature sexually. Then, greater levels of either competition or physical attraction clearly came into play depending on the sex of the parties, encouraging the older dog to sit up, take notice and start reacting one way or the other.

Choosing the second dog

It's the choice of the second dog that will determine whether the existing dog benefits or suffers from its arrival in the pack, especially the older dog. Introductions are always far more likely to be successful if a dog or puppy of the opposite sex is chosen, as this removes any likelihood that the dogs may compete, which may be quite probable with two males, especially when the puppy starts to enter puberty and perhaps challenge the old boy for position long before he is ready to abdicate. Problems are less likely when introducing another bitch to an existing female, but occasionally severe difficulties can occur when the young pup has her first season, as this can be seen as a huge social challenge to the older dog, especially if she herself is fertile. But, by and large, even members of the same sex will sort out their relationship and develop a hierarchy that enables them to enjoy each other's company.

If the new arrival is of the same breed as the first, the potential for social misunderstandings will be reduced compared with taking a totally different and perhaps less or different socially sensitive dog who might want to compete about different symbols of status. For example, a young Jack Russell might parade a stick as a trophy and symbol of his increasing importance to an older German Shepherd Dog who couldn't care less about sticks, but who will firmly put him in his place if he dares to push ahead of him going through a doorway. This is an act which an eager darting Jack Russell, even after several attacks, may never appreciate as challenging to his packmate's rank because such things are not important to Jack Russells. But, Jack Russells are made of plucky stuff and, size notwithstanding, will go down fighting even against larger and stronger opposition, inflicting painful ripostes all the way, which will not be pleasurable for the old dog.

The end result is confusion all round and two dogs who simply never trust each other and spend their days growling at every move the other makes. The impact on the old German Shepherd Dog is a severe reduction in the quality of life when his owners just wanted to keep him happy and young at heart!. But this is to paint a picture of a rare and unlikely prospect of disaster. Most Jack Russells and German Shepherd Dogs get along fine because, even with their differences in how they view their social standing, they are able to communicate well enough to get along and benefit from each other's company.

Perhaps more important when considering a companion for the older dog is to make sure that the new arrival will not grow up to be larger and thus more likely to cause hurt in play. All things considered, the best recommendation would be to get a second dog of the same breed, or one of similar sensitivity to social issues that uses the same types of language (perhaps one within the same broad grouping such as a West Highland White Terrier as a companion for a Cairn Terrier, or a Husky for a Chow for example), or one that will be roughly the same size or slightly smaller when adult, and who is of the opposite sex to the existing dog. In this case one would expect to neuter the new arrival as soon as recommended by the vet, especially if the older dog is still fertile!

LOSS OF A PACK MEMBER

If the addition of a new dog to the pack can be of benefit to the older dog, the death of an existing pack member can equally have an enormous impact on the behaviour of a dog of any age, and especially on an older dog that loses a lifelong or very close companion.

In the *Dogs Today* survey, we asked owners about the reactions of their dogs to the death of other dogs in the household. One hundred and sixty (46 per cent) of owners owned dogs that had experienced a canine bereavement but interestingly for an animal as dependent on social relations as a dog, 59 (37 per cent) showed no reaction and seemed not to notice the passing of a companion. Some owners mentioned that they had several dogs and so the impact of losing one was not so great on the others as the loss of a sole companion might have been, and perhaps any effects that may have occurred were swamped in the complications of all the other relationships in the pack. Loss of a pack member might also be expected to have less of an impact on some of the less socially conscious breeds, such as the Norfolk Terrier, compared with the the very socially organized Spitz breeds, Border Collies or German Shepherds, who, in a pack comprising dogs of the same breed, may well have to make some major rearrangements to their social order, particularly after a high-ranking member passes away.

Re-arranging the pack order

In these types of packs especially, the positions of the remaining dogs within the pack may have to alter enormously after the loss of a pack member in order to achieve a new stability. The new order will only develop perhaps after a series of power struggles between the surviving higher-ranking dogs, but every dog's character and every pair of relationships is likely to change during the post loss period as the social order adjusts and new allegiances must be formed, not only amongst the dogs, but also involving the human members of the pack. Some of the comments in the survey comments backed up these observations: 'My other dogs started fighting when old dog died'; 'He was desolate and took some time to become top dog,' (perhaps because he didn't really want to assume the mantle of responsibility). Others felt more vulnerable to possible canine challenges from outside their immediate pack – 'he became aggressive to outside dogs,' said one.

Effects of bereavement

For packs of a mix of breeds or types, the effects of bereavement will depend on how socially minded the respective dogs were and, in pairs of dogs, more on the nature of their individual relationship whatever their breed's underlying dependency on living in a defined social order. Some dogs, after all, just don't like each other much and simply come to a relationship based on mutual tolerance in their human pack, each perhaps bonding closely to a different person in the family. The loss of a barely acknowledged housemate that a dog reacts little with when alive is unlikely to cause much disturbance or distress to the survivor, who simply carries on with life as he did before.

But several dogs were also obviously relieved at the loss of a domineering or overpowering character who had assumed control of their pack, perhaps because it was important to his breed, and immediately and calmly began to enjoy a more relaxed, less military regime after the old general had gone and blossomed under the sole attention of their owners. And for others, the sense of loss may be short lived and appear almost callous, as with the owner who reported, 'He missed the other dog until the rabbit season started'!

Of the other 101 (63 per cent) cases reported in the survey, reactions in surviving dogs to loss of a canine companion ranged from 'bewildered' to 'did not eat for days', and from 'refused food and wanted to be with us all the time for about a week' to 'devastated'. Many dogs were quiet and withdrawn or appeared very lonely, and perhaps spent time looking for the other dog around the home and garden. Twelve owners said that their dog became depressed and moped around, unwilling to join in family activities and reluctant to go for a walk or play.

For some, this period of observable reaction lasted a few days or a week, after which the survivor got slowly back in to the swing of life, but others took far longer to return to anything like their old selves. 'He mourned for 6 months,' wrote one owner, while another said 'he became more attached to us and wouldn't be left on his own afterwards' indicating the huge impact on a dog's self-confidence that suddenly losing a companion can have. Without the option of human company, this bereaved dog would be highly likely to show the usual signs of separation anxiety (*see* p. 78), but with a level of distress and intensity of reaction that would be extremely difficult to treat.

A dog that obviously enjoys a close lifelong relationship with another, such as when littermates are kept together into adulthood, can be expected to suffer enormously if its companion dies. Owners can predict this, as one survey respondent wrote of her German Shepherd Dogs 'Boris' and 'Igor'. Although neither dog showed much reaction when her other dog had died earlier, she anticipated great problems when the time came for Boris or Igor. 'When Boris went to the vet for minor surgery, Igor was distraught and chewed a hole in the back door,' she wrote, but knowing in advance that problems are inevitable does not necessarily make it any easier to plan what to do in such circumstances. In as much as death is unavoidable, so too is bereavement and grief in so many cases and most us just have to try and work our way through the mourning process and help our dogs to do so as best we can.

Behaviour changes

Psychologically, many dogs reacted very badly to their loss, showing marked behaviour changes such as increased reactivity shown largely by barking loudly at every slight disturbance. Others engaged in frequent bouts of distressed howling, perhaps in a vain effort to make contact with a packmate which the dog thought might just have strayed away from the den and got lost, a logical enough idea when you have no concept of death and backed up by the fact that several dogs in the survey took up positions by the door or garden gate as if waiting for their companion to return. One howler quickly overcame his distress and stopped his crying when a new puppy was introduced, but for others, the grief they felt was intense, traumatic and not so simple to ease. After all, how does one explain the concept of death to a creature to help it come to terms with its pain when it has even less of an idea of what death entails than we have, but yet which can suffer from the effects of bereavement probably as much as we do?

One poor dog reported in the survey suffered two strokes after losing a companion and the particularly sad comments of, 'We thought he would die of heartache,' and 'We nearly lost him as well,' came from owners who must have been beside themselves trying to cope with their dog's reactions on top of their own to the loss of their friend. One dog, who lost her brother suddenly, aged prematurely in her shock at his death, going grey around the muzzle and even now, two years on, is rather subdued, and behaves as a much older and vulnerable dog, continuing to wake her owner for reassurance during the night.

For other dogs the anxiety and vulnerability that can follow the loss of a canine friend caused more involuntary reactions with 'soiling' and 'wetting' occurring in the dog's bed. More deliberate territorial marking with urine, both indoors and outdoors was reported in a few cases. This would presumably help the survivor reinforce his own sense of security by surrounding himself with his own scent at a time when he felt himself to be vulnerable.

Dealing with loss

While temporary loss of appetite is a common feature of many bereaved social animals, it usually lasts only a few days and causes no long-term harm. But some dogs appeared to be so unwell after the death of a companion that their owners sought veterinary advice. Long-term depression and loss of appetite to the point where the dog loses condition and even starts to waste away can often be helped with the prescription of a little low-dose Valium by the vet. This helps the disturbed or depressed dog relax and thus stimulates appetite which in turn gives them more energy and enthusiasm to get back into the swing of things again. Many 'alternative' remedies such as homoeopathic and Bach's Flower remedies can also be helpful with bereaved dogs and their owners, but ideally should only be used when 'prescribed' by a veterinary or medical practitioner with a special interest and knowledge in the subject.

Helping dogs overcome their sense of loss can require lots of TLC, time free of other stresses or, for some dogs, the acquisition of another dog. One of the best things to do for many bereaved people and dogs is to take a holiday, encounter mild new challenges and develop new social contacts that make restoring one's usual approach to life easier, and then return, psychologically stronger, to dealing with all those reminders back home. The canine spirit is usually strong and they will get over their grief.

9. Old age comforts

While our older cats can usually find a cosy spot of their own choosing, be it the windowsill on a sunny day or the airing cupboard in a blizzard, our dogs have to rely on us to provide them with warmth and comfort. Many old dogs also feel more vulnerable and less confident. They constantly follow their owners around and may not actually sleep until their owner sits down or at least stays in one place for a long period of time. They may need two, three or more beds in different rooms so they can relax while keeping their beloved owners in view.

Where to put the bed

There are several factors to consider when choosing a bed (or beds) and the position for it (or them). Beds needs to be out of drafts which could chill those old bones and make joints even more painful. Normal changes during ageing affect the body's ability to thermoregulate quite so efficiently and thinning of the coat cuts down on the body's natural insulation. Perhaps that bed near the back door where the young dog used to flop when he came in wet and muddy after a really active walk needs to be moved to a cosy corner. Old dogs are more sensitive to extremes of cold or hot, so the really steaming spot next to the boiler may be too hot, although many oldies happily spend their days in front of the fire or next to the radiator in cold weather. Raising a bed slightly off the floor and adding 'sides' or draught blockers will help to cut out those sharp little darts of cold air.

Bed size and shape

Because dogs may not be as supple as they were, the size or shape of the bed may need to be changed. Older dogs may want to stretch out rather than curl up as they can 'seize up' in certain positions. Because the muscle has lost tone and joints are a bit creaky, the body is less able to support itself – there is less 'give' and bony elbows and joints tend to poke out more sharply. If the dog is sleeping on a hard surface or a thin bed the pressure on these points can be very painful and callouses can form. Of course, the bigger and heavier the dog, the more problems it will have. It may be time to reasses the bed, make it thicker and enlarge it so that the dog can stretch out. Some older dogs seem to like to lie on their backs – perhaps taking the weight off their feet altogether. Putting a bed in a corner also gives support and protection. There are numerous dog beds available on the market for all sizes of canines; larger dogs may appreciate one of those huge beanbags which mould to the shape of their body so providing firm support while still being comfortable. An old mattress will let them stretch out in comfort – if the house is big enough! Extra blankets, cushions or Vetbed (another very warm fleecy type of bedding which can be easily washed, address on pp. 121) will all be appreciated.

If the dog is unsettled because he feels unsure about being separated from his owner at night it may be time to think about putting a bed in or near the bedroom and then everyone can relax – as long as the dog doesn't snore! There may, of course, be problems if the house is on several levels and the oldie cannot manage the stairs.

If there are young children in the house the dog may want somewhere to 'get away from it all' and relax without the constant patting and attention which toddlers think every person and every animal must love as much as them.

An indoor kennel

Wherever the bed or beds are placed, they should afford an undisturbed rest for the older dog. After all, the older the dog becomes, the more time he will spend in his beds resting and he needs very much to feel that his bed is his den and affords similar security and comfort to a hole in the ground. This may be the reason some dogs prefer to sleep in corners or under tables and like the security and support of having a solid surface against their backs. Indeed, while many pet behaviourists and vets now recommend the use of indoor mesh kennels for puppies, both in terms of providing a safe den area and helping with house training, many also recommend their use for older dogs. The protection and physical support afforded by the bars of the pen helps many older dogs relax better, even if the door is left open and they can enter and leave at will. At any time when they feel tired or insecure, or simply want to get out of the way of busy household goings-on without sleeping but still keeping an eye on things, the collapsible mesh pen is perfect. And, as most are readily transportable, they can also be moved to the car, hotels, kennels, friends' houses etc to transfer the feeling of having access to a secure den in perhaps otherwise unfamiliar surroundings and making such temporary upheavals easier to deal with for the older dog.

Lighting the way

Many old people do not sleep well at night so we should not be surprised if some owners find their older dogs are unsettled in the wee small hours. A quick visit to the garden to relieve the bladder and a reassuring pat, is all that most need before they settle down again. One owner wrote, 'On the rare occasion that she needs to go out in the middle of the night I have to go accompany her round the garden in my nightie because her night sight is so poor.' Oldies would probably appreciate one of those really bright outdoor lights which come on automatically when someone goes into the garden so they don't trip over the flowerbeds or pots in the middle of the night.

Warm and dry

Make sure the dog is towel-dried after a wet walk and its bed is kept dry, as dampness creeps into old joints and bones, making life very miserable. The sparser, less oily coat of the older dog has reduced water repellant qualities and can let the damp seep right through. Unattended long coats dry much less quickly because the mats of hair can soak up water – as well as being uncomfortable to lie on. A quick blow dry with the hair drier can speed up the drying process.

For very chilly pooches try wrapping a water bottle in a towel or putting a heated pad under the blankets. The heater is a metal pad which is plugged it into the mains (available from Petnap, *see* address on p. 125) – it is appropriate for the smaller breeds but not really large enough for a Labrador or Wolfhound and certainly not for the inveterate chewer.

Materials are also available which reflect the dog's body heat and building up a warm 'nest' of air around the animal. This material is used in bedding by a company called Serendipity in their Flectabed (for address *see* p. 121) which has an inner quilt with contains Flectalon and separate fleecy outer cover which allows moisture to pass through. Flectalon is said to prevent vital heat loss by reflecting back over 90 per cent of the dog's own body heat. Again it is machine washable.

Some breeds feel the cold so much more than others – Dobermanns are well known as 'heat-seeking missiles' in the winter. Their coat does not have that soft under-layer of fur which helps to trap the air providing a warm layer – without it, the heat from the body is soon lost. Compare the Dobermann's coat to that of a Husky or Newfoundland, natives of the frozen climes, and you will realise why these sleek dogs are usually to be found next to the best source of heat in the house from early autumn to late spring. Dobermanns and other single-coated breeds can really feel the cold in the winter and many owners of this lovely breed (often thought of as fierce!) tuck their shivering pet into bed in the winter snuggled in duvets with blankets over the top!

Leaky problems

In chapter 5, the causes of incontinence are discussed and it can be a huge problem or just a mild irritation depending on the severity of the problem. A company called OTT Textiles (address on p. 121) produces a hygienic pad in several different sizes to suit most dogs. The pad has a 'stay dry' surface and liquids drain into highly absorbent wadding – ideal for dogs which are incontinent or just a little bit 'leaky' or are recovering from surgery. It seems to be an ideal solution as it can be put over the dog's favourite chair or beanbag or even just on the floor in front of the fire, saving the furniture or carpet and allowing the dog to maintain all the comforts it has become used to. The car interior could also benefit. The pad can be machine washed and put in the tumble drier.

Barka Parka make a Dri-Top cover which goes underneath the washable slip-cover on their bean bags and protects the bed from dampness or soiling. (address on p. 121. Alternatively some owners visit their local jumble sales regularly and keep a supply of old blankets and sheets which they can wash until they fall apart and then replace at little cost.

One lady even placed special rubber lined absorbent bedding on the dog's side of her bed 'to keep him dry when he wets himself', so carrying management of the geriatric dog into the realms of human intensive care. But another owner described how she now always gave her elderly dog 'breakfast in bed before he gets up' and surely none of us would raise any objection to being treated to that level of compassion in our old age!

Coat care

Grooming has two very important uses; not only does it ensure the coat is kept free from tangles, but dogs enjoy the attention and physical contact – it helps maintain the bond between owner and dog which seems to be especially important to the oldies. In chapter 2 the changes which occur in the skin and coat were outlined. Grooming can help stimulate blood flow to the skin and hair follicles, which may help to spread the oil from the sebaceous glands along the hairs, improve waterproofing qualities of the coat and keeping the skin supple. Dogs with thin coats may benefit from a doggy coat on winter outings – there are all sorts of coats available, from fur-lined 'anoraks' to waxed jackets.

Older dogs are less able to cope with infection or the annoyance of parasites so grooming is an ideal opportunity to give the dog a once over to check for lumps and bumps (*see* tumours in chapter 5). This can be particularly important in the summer when grass seeds can become lodged in the coat or between the dog's toes. These seeds can actually work their way into the flesh and track up the leg or into the body and cause serious problems.

Check between the toes and in the ears, especially in long-haired breeds. Matted hair not only makes seed retention more likely, but the actual bulk of hair can make the dog uncomfortable, especially if the lumps of hair build up between the toes. The smoothies too will benefit from an invigorating brush which may relieve a few itches, especially if the coat is becoming a little dry.

While we usually think about keeping our oldies warm, some of the heavy coated breeds can become too hot in warm weather. Old dogs find it hard to cope with excess heat and those with heavy coats may benefit from being clipped during the summer months. Heavy dogs may have callouses on their elbows because they lie on hard surfaces. These can crack, become infected, causing pain and discomfort. Rubbing Vaseline on them can help to keep them soft and supple, but always check with your vet if there is any inflammation. New hair can re-grow if the callouses are treated and the animal given somewhere soft to lie.

Nails

Because older dogs are less active, their nails are unlikely to be worn down naturally and will need to be clipped. They become more brittle in old age and because they crack and flake, are more likely to get caught in carpets or furnishings. This can result in a sharp jolt for the dog as it is stopped suddenly in its tracks. The nail bed itself can also become injured.

Long nails can cause problems walking because the dog is not resting its weight on the pad of its paws but being rocked back by the long nails which hit the floor first. A dog which is already a bit wobbly may find this unnerving or even painful if it has joint or back troubles.

If you have problems cutting your dog's claws try doing it after a bath when the nails are more pliable. There are some very good dog nail clippers on the market which make the job fairly easy, but if you have real problems your vet will do the job for you. As is the case with most grooming practices, if it is begun in puppyhood the dog accepts it as normal and will not object to it in later life.

Bath time

Old dogs can get a bit on the 'smelly' side and may be relieved to have a warm bath to clean them up and remove itches. If you are using the bath make sure you have a rubber mat for the dog to stand on so it can relax and not slip and slide. Use mild shampoos or flea treatments – check with your vet if you have any worries – as some products may cause skin irritation. Dry the dog carefully to ensure it does not get chilled.

Slippery surfaces

Although a highly polished floor may look beautiful and its slippery surface delightful for a puppy to slide about on, for the older dog it is definitely a 'no-go-zone'. Old dogs do have the sense to avoid places where they cannot get any grip with their feet and may simply refuse to walk on that floor. If they do they may come to a shaky standstill, becoming tense and distressed because they feel so unsure of their footing. Old dogs' pads are usually fairly dry and cracked and their nails may be a little too long so that they have no purchase on the floor at all. Slithering about and falling can be quite a shock to the system and may be the last straw for a dog which is just about coping with locomotion problems. Larger dogs in particular can become very worried if they cannot grip. If the dog has to cross a particular floor which is polished or even slightly slippery, put a carpet, rug or runner across it so he can wander across in safety.

Stairs

Stairs can also pose a great problem for dogs when they become old. If your dog is small or you are strong and fit you may be able to carry it up and down if necessary but this is not really an option for the larger breeds. One of the owners who replied to our survey wrote that her dog had died because it had fallen down the stairs when it was 14. Often dogs manage to get up but overbalance on the way down. Putting a stair gate at the bottom to stop the dog going up can give you peace of mind – think of it as having a toddler all over again!

EXERCISE

Many older dogs become stiff during or after walks – this usually occurs at about 10 or 11 years. Many are fine while actually out on their walks but have problems getting up after a sleep when they get home. By 13 or 14 years old almost all dogs suffer mobility problems such as stiffness/weak legs, wobbly back end, breathing problems, slowing or lagging behind during a walk or just getting 'dog tired'. It is important not to give up exercise and feel that old Fido can just lie around in his bed all day; he may only go a short distance but it will keep his muscles and joints more supple and add interest to his day.

Keen joggers may have to take stock of their pet's age a little sooner than the slower walkers. A fast pace and pounding the ground may be too much for the heavier breeds or those with short legs and while they enjoyed the exercise as pups and young dogs, it is now becoming too much for them. Remember, too, that while you have super air-cushioned shoes which act as shock absorbers and foot protectors, the pads of a dog's feet can become worn and sore and a hard surface may also damage the dog's joints.

Don't overdo it

Some dogs, of course, are so enthusiastic that they forget the messages that their bodies give them during or after long walks and bounce around as much as ever they did at the sound of the lead or the appearance of the walking shoes and coat, only remembering that it isn't so easy any more when half way across the park. It's vital that owners keep a close eye on the true capabilities of their dogs at this stage and don't let them overdo it. While some dogs need a fair amount of encouragement to get out of their cosy beds and keep active and will benefit from frequent short walks, other highly active types, particularly the working breeds such as spaniels and collies, need to be protected from an enthusiasm which can often remain undaunted by age and physical decline. Short and frequent walks, some restrained on a long lead perhaps, followed by opportunity for quiet undisturbed rest back home and interspersed with lots of gentle ball games in the garden and more indoor games and social contact may help the older dog adjust without suffering from trying to continue with an old 'hell-for-leather' attitude to life that might otherwise be leading to physical problems and strain ageing muscles and the heart.

Conditioned by years of two robust runs a day at the same times, the older dog will surely be confused if one walk is suddenly curtailed and so it is usually best to stick to the same routines of going out, but to shorten the circuit and throw the ball less along the way. Later, it may be possible to keep the dog on the lead for a longer period of the walk, or put him back on the lead occasionally and walk at a gentler pace to enable him to get his breath back fully from previous exertions. And as time marches on, it may be wise to introduce shorter walks in between the established ones, both to help spread the exercise more evenly and avoid the undue strains of long walks and to help manage other problems, such any developing urinary incontinence by getting the dog out more.

Encouraging play

Keeping active ensures that the dog retains its interest in life, and exercise helps prevent the whole system from 'rusting up'. But what sort of activity? Indoors there are lots of games to play, many of which the dog will already have enjoyed as a puppy, such as hunting the concealed toy or titbit. Beware, though, of tugging games with delicate jaws and loose or missing teeth and avoid wrestling games with old bodies, no matter how willing the ageing Boxer or Rottweiler may be to test his strength.

Being able to encourage the older dog to play reminds us both of when life was easier for him and keeps his mind alert and his body as fit and supple as his condition will now allow. It's vital that we continue to encourage a dog to play in old age, even if a couple of retrieves are all he can manage, so that a good quality of life is maintained for him as long as possible.

For dogs who are still active and willing to play and who will do anything they can that might bring rewards, controlling the availability of food can be very useful way of keeping minds and bodies active. Offering food in several small meals will keep them listening out for the food bowl, while hiding the food in a room before allowing the dog access will also keep the 'hunting' instincts sharp, even if they might need a little help in the form of a food trail (best with dry 'complete' foods or mixer biscuits rather than wet or canned meats!) to find the bowl. Pointing or verbal instructions such as 'left, right, good, no, yes, yes, bingo!' might also help as senses decline, or frustration at not finding the food may cause the older dog to give up looking rather than heightening the desire to look harder.

For the fit but elderly dog who cannot manage a full blown romp around the fields every day, mental and physical stimulation can be provided outdoors by distributing one or more meals (again, the most effective and hygienic are 'complete' dry diets) from the daily rations around the lawn and leaving the dog to track down each nugget. This may keep the dog thoroughly occupied for an hour or more and while he will locate and consume the first nine tenths of the food quickly, he will carry on looking for the rest for a long time afterwards at a much lower strike rate.

Care is needed for the very hungry or enthusiastic dog put to this natural scavenging ritual as they will not be aware when they have consumed the last nugget and will stay out looking for it for ever unless brought in! Such activity not only keeps the dog moving and gently exercised over a long period but also serves to keep the senses of smell and vision exercised.

Travel

For some dogs travel is a necessity in order to go for walks or as part of their daily routine in travelling everywhere with their owners. For others it is an occasional trip, often to the vet. Small dogs pose no problems if they need some help in getting into the car, but the large breeds may no longer spring into the boot in one athletic bound but become stuck half way there. Jumping in or out on to hard ground can be difficult and painful, so you may need to provide a ramp or steps for a more graceful and less dramatic performance. You may even want to think about a doggy harness (such as a seat belt, *see* address on pp. 121) which will prevent the dog being thrown about in the car, or put some cushions in the back so that the dog does not keep hitting itself against hard edges if its balance isn't as good as it was.

Take great care when the weather is hot – many dogs still die in cars in the warm weather. Old dogs have more difficulty regulating their temperature and will be more easily affected by heat stroke. Leaving them in the car on an even moderately warm or sunny day may no longer be an option.

WHEN YOU GO ON HOLIDAY

One dilemma, which faces both dog and cat owners, is what to do with their animals when they go on holiday. Some people, worried that their dog will pine or become ill if it goes into a kennel while they are away, simply decide to stay at home. But will an older dog really be upset by having to go into a boarding kennel? The answer very much depends on the individual personality of the dog and its ability to cope with change or stress. Certainly, change is more difficult for older animals to cope with, just as it is for older people and there is no doubt most would prefer to stay in their own homes. However, if the dog has been using a local kennel for many years and knows the people and the routine there, then it may not be over-stressed by the change of venue and will settle down happily and watch proceedings with a seasoned eye.

Choosing a kennel

Putting an old dog into a kennel for the first time late in its life, however, may prove more stressful. The worry can be greatly decreased if you know that the kennel is clean, efficient and caring. Good kennels are often found by word of mouth, but if you have no recommendations then go along yourself and have a look around. If the people in charge do not want you to see beyond the reception area, assume they have something to hide, go home and choose another kennel to inspect. A good kennel proprietor will know that the oldie has special needs and will take careful note of all your instructions. The kennel should be able to provide a heating lamp if the dog feels the cold and ensure the dog has its special diet or medication as necessary. Of course, it is up to you to ensure that specific instructions are given in writing, and that the name and address of the dog's vet are enclosed, along with permission for the kennel owner to request veterinary help if necessary.

Dog-sitters

Most old dogs would undoubtedly prefer to stay at home when you go away, so if you are only absent for a short time you may have a friend who can come and stay. It may be worthwhile seeking out a reputable dog or house sitter who will come to your home and look after the dog's every need there.

Naturally such services are more expensive than a kennel, but they also give you peace of mind about house security. Good service usually spreads by word of mouth and most sitters will give you references. One long established firm of house sitters is called Home Sitters (*see* address on p. 121). They will send you their guidelines for both sitters and owners, and provide a service all over the country. There may also be more local sitters in your own area: addresses are usually found in the pet magazines or local papers. Ask for references and check up on them yourself.

Moving house

Not only do some people not go on holiday when they have an older dog, some actually decide they are not going to move house until the dog has gone. Undoubtedly moving house would be stressful to a very old dog as routine and feeling at home are very important. However, while your old dog may be creaky and seem to be on his last legs at 12, he may go on for three or four years more at least and there may be no option but to move. Try and make it as smooth as possible and put the old pooch in a comfortable warm room with all his bits and pieces around, plus one of your old unwashed jumpers or tee shirts which will comfort him. Then the usual moving chaos can go on all around that little oasis of peace.

Ins and outs

If your dog stays in all day while you are at work and has to wait to spend a penny until you come home, you may have to make a few adjustments if the dog is having problems crossing his legs all day. Because the kidney is less efficient at concentrating urine, a larger volume is produced, and because all the muscles are a little slacker, the dog may not be able to 'hold on' and may become stressed waiting for your return. If a helpful neighbour is not available to let the dog out occasionally during the day, consider installing a dog door – the canine equivalent of a cat flap. They are available in several sizes, so most sizes of dog can be catered for.

Of course, the larger the dog door the more likely it is that a person could get through, so security must be considered too. You will also need a very escape-proof garden if the dog is to be out without escort. Safety for house and dog are obviously the most important considerations, but a flap could relieve not only the dog but worried owner too. A door may also let the dog go out at night without the need for you to rise from your warm and cosy bed. If you are going to install a flap make sure that there is not too big a drop on the outside as this could make life difficult for the stiff dog – add a step or two on either side if necessary. (*See* address for Staywell Pet Doors, p. 121).

Eating and drinking

Often it is the simple things in life which can be the most helpful. Raising a dish or water bowl so that the dog does not have to bend down too far to eat or drink may be a great relief to a large dog or one with neck or back problems. You can make your own device or buy one (*see* address for Luxway Canine supplies, p. 121). Make sure too that the old dog does not have to run the gauntlet of younger, fitter canines, or even a despotic cat, in order to get to food or water.

COPING WITH PHYSICAL PROBLEMS

Many people are shocked when their vet tells them that their dog is going blind or deaf, or will have to have a limb removed. They worry about about how their pet will manage and if they can cope with it. Some owners decide that they do not wish their animal to suffer the trauma of an operation, or realise that they cannot give it the attention it will need with a disability. Others decide to nurse their pets.

Blindness

Whereas blind and deaf cats are not that common, dogs with impaired sight are fairly plentiful. Dogs seem to start having sight problems at about 10 or 11 years old and if they live to 14 or more, undoubtedly have some sort of trouble seeing (*see* chapter 5 for an explanation of the causes of blindness). As loss of sight is often a slow process, dogs can compensate fairly well as long they they stick to routines and places they know. Blind people will tell you that their senses of hearing, touch and smell become more acute and that they rely on these other senses much more than fully sighted people. No doubt the same is true for dogs, although the very old ones are more than likely to be having hearing problems too.

Learning new signals

It can often help with older dogs to precede times of enjoyable things such as physical contact, play, exercise and feeding with a signal, perhaps a bell, as used in Pavlov's famous experiments with dogs in the 1920s. His studies showed that a response to something pleasurable, such as salivation before being fed, could become conditioned to an uninvolved signal, such as the ring of a bell, if the sound coincided with the presentation of the food.

If we precede one or two things that the old dog enjoys, such as being fed or having the door opened to be allowed out into the garden, by ringing a low-pitched bell (older dogs tend to lose the top end of the hearing range as their inner ear seizes up a little and so usually hear better at the lower end of the scale), we can soon use the sound of the bell to call the dog to us for other activities. This can help to keep the dog moving and socially involved in the latter stages of life when he otherwise might choose not to leave his bed. This form of communication will work so long as the dog can hear the sound (though other signals can also be used, such as stamping the feet to cause vibration or flashing a light or camera flash) providing of course that we continue to reward the dog's response with the occasional food treat and/or a welcoming pat or one of the original pleasurable events that the signal was paired with.

Reassurance as sight fails

Clearly verbal contact and perhaps the use of other conditioning sounds such as John Fisher's famous brass Dog Training Discs, (usually employed to speed and simplify basic training or in the treatment of specific behaviour problems, *see* address on p. 121) become all the more important for the older dog that loses his sight. It is important for owners to remember that as the older dog loses the ability to see his owners and interpret their body language and follow their movements, levels of verbal communication and reassurance through touch need to be stepped up to compensate. And, even as a dog will probably demand more time of his owners in caring for him medically in old age, more time is also required in communicating with him.

The best thing to do is keep talking and introduce new signals to the older dog with failing eyesight before he loses it altogether, as old signals can be more readily exchanged for new ones while they are still operative. Many dogs become much more vocal as they age and the senses of hearing and vision mainly used in communication with people decline. (Though dogs use their sense of smell in communication with us as well as other dogs, they have usually realised long ago that our sense of smell is far too poor to be used in the context of social investigation and identity). But with sight and hearing limited, even if we are speaking louder and more frequently to our old dogs, they attempt, sometimes desperately to ensure that we are aware of their presence by barking, whining and howling. And when those key senses have gone, only the response of touch and opportunity to sniff our hands at close quarters will reassure the dog that we are near and still looking after them.

By this stage, it's pointless to suggest that we are in danger of encouraging over-attachment if we respond to every noise – we are in the final stages of our relationship, when the dog really does need constant care and contact from us and we should be there to offer it. Leaving a short trailing lead on the dog can help at this stage as this can simply be stepped on or picked up, establishing a social link indoors to reassure the dog even when we are otherwise occupied and can't offer our full attention.

Touch is important

Touch naturally also becomes increasingly important to the older dog. It provides reassurance in a social context with packmates and helps him relate to the environment. This is especially the case with dogs whose senses of vision, smell and hearing are on the wane. While it may be difficult with smaller breeds and types of dog, larger dogs with visual and or hearing disabilities should be frequently touched when walking to maintain contact, and given plenty of opportunity to lie up next to you when everyone is resting.

Not that you may have a lot of choice in the matter. One owner in the *Dogs Today* survey wrote, 'If I am sitting, you won't find her on the floor! I have to sew, write etc over the top of her or resting on her back.' Another, clearly enjoying the reassuring feelings of touching a smaller canine friend herself, told how, 'She now spends hours asleep on my knee.'

It also helps, of course, not to move furniture or fixtures in the home or garden of dogs with fading eyesight or, if that is unavoidable, to take the dog to the area so that he can touch and smell that things have changed. Dogs do seem remarkably resilient to bangs on the face and falling over when their eyesight is poor, but if you know your dog's sight is failing, walk and run him off lead in large open areas so that he can get to know the geography of the place and continue to enjoy running even after his sight has failed completely, relying on his mental map and senses of smell, hearing and touch. That way, there will be no loss of exercise or enjoyment of life for an otherwise healthy active dog

Replacement whiskers

While blind cats seem to be able to act fairly normally and can even hunt provided the quarry does not fly off the ground, dogs do not seem to have the same feline touch sensitivity or 'sixth sense' and are much more likely to bumble about and fall over things! The cat's whiskers can sometimes be thought of as a third eye – the cat can even feel changes in the movement of air around itself as well as closer objects which actually hit its whiskers.

Richard Ettelson, a farmer in West Virginia took the principle of whiskers a little further some years ago. He had noticed that his blind Labrador Cinder had worn out her whiskers and her muzzle had become sore because she kept bumping into things. She had also fallen off the porch steps. He decided to give Cinder new 'whiskers; by mounting two flexible canes on her collar, pointing forward so that they ended a couple of inches beyond the front of the dog's nose. The canes had to be flexible enough to bend so as to avoid being caught up in chair legs and to enable the dog to lie comfortably. In two weeks Cinder had learned to feel the changes in pressure against the collar and associate scraping noises with obstacles. She no longer fell off the porch and learned to keep her head down – when the floor dropped away at steps, she stopped. To avoid those small objects which might be missed by the canes, Cinder learned to walk in a diagonal pattern to sweep the area ahead.

The design was further modified by a veterinary nurse called Sue Parry who found that the prongs bent too easily. She attached a continuous piece of light, pliable but strong plastic (about 4 cm wide) to the collar so that it forms a bow in front of the dog's head. Judy. the Jack Russell who wears the device successfully negotiates all sorts of obstacles including a maze of bar stools at the local pub seeking out sympathetic people with crisps (her senses of hearing and smell are still fine!). She wears it at a high angle because she goes along with her nose on the ground and the bow alerts her that there are objects in her path.

Familiar surroundings

A blind dog, just like a blind person, gets to know its way around the furniture in the house or the layout of the garden. This means it is best to try and keep everything in the same place so it does not have to relearn the route all the time. Remember, too, that a blind dog will rely more on its sense of smell than before, so it is necessary to be aware of how changing smells will affect it. Compared to the dog, man has a very poor sense of smell indeed, you only have to use your imagination to realise that a new carpet could completely disorientate the blind animal for a few days, because its strong smell may overwhelm the familiar smells of the furnishings along the routes it usually takes. The dog will have a smell profile of its home, just as we would have a visual plan of our house in our minds. Change this by moving furniture around and you will not only affect the dog physically, but may disorientate it mentally by altering this olfactory plan.

Your presence will be of great importance to the blind dog. In the wild, dogs survive in packs and the presence of other pack members is important to well-being as well as survival. If your dog cannot see the rest of its pack (i.e. you) it will be worried. It will hear and smell you and will learn to pinpoint you by your voice, so don't let the fact that your dog cannot see you keep you from talking to it. Some simple rules and props will enable you and the dog to form a routine that allows a normal life. One lady wrote of the importance of routine to her old dog: 'She knows our routine and makes sure we stick to it – we'd need to get a clock if we didn't have her.'

Blind dogs or those with impaired vision may be wary of going out and may need to be kept on a lead for their own safety. One lady with a fairly blind Jack Russell Terrier said that her dog would follow any pair of legs on a walk. Putting the dog on a long lead, such as a Flexilead (address on p. 125), will enable it to saunter along, but be rescueable if necessary. This is even more important if the dog is deaf as well.

DEAFNESS

Many owners are very surprised to find that their dog has lost its sense of hearing, because this can be such a gradual process. Usually the dog has compensated over the years and now copes well. They may have felt a little 'put out' that the dog does not come when it is called or wake from sleep when they enter the room but, over the years, they have probably attributed this to stubbornnes or laziness. It is only when a third party – often the vet – points the deafness out that everything makes sense. They realise their pet has actually been coping with a handicap remarkably well and is not really stubborn. Sometimes the presence of a second dog in the house completely masks a hearing problem as the deaf dog merely barks when its companion barks and runs to the door and generally becomes excited at the same time. It is only when the companion has died or is absent for a long period that the dog notices its cues are no longer there.

Non-verbal communication

The onset of sensory deficiencies makes it important to introduce new signals of communication for the previously relied on verbal commands of 'come', 'sit' and 'lie down', – even if 'stay' is now what the dog has decided to do most readily. At the first sign of failing hearing, hand and body signals and other visual signals such as light flashes, plus perhaps different audible signals based on lower pitched noises and vibrations, should be introduced and interspersed with the verbal instructions. Then they can replace them fully in later years, maintaining contact and reassurance for the dog if he does become deaf. Even so, getting a deaf dog's attention while out on a walk can be very difficult and it is probably safer to keep it on a long flexible lead – if its nose is in the grass it won't see your hand signals. If your oldie is on the bad-tempered side avoid startling him by suddenly touching him – move his sleeping place out of the main thoroughfare.

DISABLED DOGS

Many old dogs become quite disabled because of joint problems, paralysis or amputation. Owners must decide whether they can cope with the problem and whether their dog is happy being helped around. It often comes down to the size of the dog and the strength of the owner. The larger the dog, the more weight the body has to support, and if its legs are not firm beneath it, the dog may feel very vulnerable.

If the condition is temporary, a clever little dog carrier could help. The Canine Helping Hand (*see* p. 125 for address) provides a way of relieving the weight normally supported by the dog's back legs while allowing the front legs to function properly. It allows the person supporting the dog's weight to stand upright and comfortable and gives the dog space to attempt to support itself. As the dog's condition improves, it can take more and more of its own weight.

Long-term solutions

Owners faced with decisions about going on with treatment should work closely with their vet who can help in assessment of pain or prognosis. If the dog has to be lifted in and out of the garden for a short period while recovering from an operation or while getting used to life on three legs, then most owners can cope. It is the more enduring injuries or illnesses which can cause problems, especially if the dog seems bright in itself but has become paralysed in its back legs.

For some dogs, the answer can lie in a canine version of a wheelchair called a K-9 Cart (address on p. 121). Consisting of a harness and wheels, the carts are custom-built for each dog to support the dog's hindquarders just off the ground – the wheels enable the dog to pull itself along and lead a fairly active life. Be guided by your vet as to whether your dog is suited to such a cart both in its condition, breed and temperament. It may not be suitable for some older dogs if they are generally weak or cannot control their bodily functions.

10. Letting go

Our dogs are part of the family and when they die we can suffer the same grief and emotions as we do when a human dies. 'My dog is like a first born child, we share love and mutal adoration,' said one owner on our survey; another commented, 'I would rather lose my house, job and all my possessions than lose Arron';another lady described her dogs as 'woven into the structure of my life'.

When our dogs become ill we do all in our power to help – usually regardless of the financial or time burdens this can bring. When the bond with our pets is put to the test we know the strength it has. Illness in a beloved and faithful old friend can bring out the best in us.

EUTHANASIA – MAKING THE DECISION

Sometimes it is obvious when the time has come to say goodbye to an ill pet. However, if the dog's health has been deteriorating slowly because of a chronic condition, it can be very difficult to know just where to draw the line. The diagnosis of a terminal condition, such as cancer, does not mean that the dog should be put to sleep immediately. With the major advances in veterinary medicine much can be done to give dogs a few more happy and pain-free months or even years of life. You will be working with your vet as a team – he or she to monitor the condition and you to watch your dog's behaviour. Over the years your dog's habits will have become familiar to you – when these patterns begin to change you may need to monitor them closely. As we have seen earlier in this book, the lifestyle of an elderly dog will gradually slow down as it ages and illness will further limit its ability to live a completely normal lifestyle. However, the crucial point comes when you must decide whether, on balance, your dog is still enjoying life. The following questions may help you to come to a decision:

- Has your dog ceased to enjoy its food?
- Does your dog no longer enjoy regular exercise?
- Has your dog stopped responding to you and your family?
- Is your dog vomiting repeatedly?
- Is your dog incontinent?
- Does your dog have severe difficulty in getting around?
- Does your dog show signs of pain or discomfort?
- Is your dog having frequent convulsions?

If the answer to one or more of these questions is 'yes' and your veterinary surgeon does not feel able to improve your dog's condition with treatment, then euthanasia should be seriously considered. Your vet is experienced in judging the longer term outlook for your dog and should be able to offer you guidance, although at the end of the day the decision has to be yours.

Although many people hope their pet will die naturally without suffering, this easy alternative does not often happen. Some dogs will experience considerable distress in their final hours, vomiting repeatedly, struggling for breath or having convulsions. When it is obvious that your dog is no longer enjoying life and veterinary medicine has no more to offer, it is kinder to take the decision yourself and have your dog put to sleep and ensure that suffering is avoided.

What happens ?

Worrying about the unknown is often worse than the actual event. Wondering what actually happens when a dog is put down or put to sleep or euthanased can trouble owners. There is no doubt you will be upset and most veterinary surgeons are very sensitive to the grief they know owners will be feeling. Many make an effort to schedule an appointment when you can bring your dog in outside the busy surgery time, so you do not have to sit in the waiting room with everyone else and try to keep yourself under control.

You may wish to have the vet visit you at home, although there is a strong argument in favour of taking your dog to the surgery where your vet can carry out the task in ideal conditions and with the nursing staff to hand. Talk to your vet and assess the pros and cons and between you decide what is best. Some owners wish to stay with their dogs, which is something most vets encourage. They feel that the dog will be more relaxed with its owner close by. Owners are often relieved to witness how quick and painless the procedure actually is. It can be very difficult to stay, but decide what you can cope with, get help if necessary, and let your vet know what you want to do.

If the recommendation that it is really best to end the dog's suffering comes as a shock to you, you may want some time to consider the matter and to prepare your family. If the dog is in distress, then it is selfish to prolong its agony, but with many conditions it is possible for your vet to administer drugs to keep the dog comfortable for another day or two, until you are ready.

How is it done?

If you decide euthanasia is the most humane choice, you may be asked to sign a form giving consent. It is almost always carried out by an injection with an overdose of barbiturate. This drug is used as an anaesthetic at lower doses and it is not unreasonable to assume that the sensation experienced by the dog is exactly the same as if an anaesthetic were being administered and it slipped into sleep.

Hair is clipped from a small area on the dog's front leg so that a vein can easily be found. The dog is held by a nurse and the drug in injected into the vein. The only thing the dog will feel is a slight prick and the effect of the injection is very fast. If the dog is very nervous the vet may give it a sedative first.

Loss of consciousness is usually immediate and very soon the heart will cease to function. It is quite common for the dog to take a gasp or two a little while afterwards and you may also notice some muscle-twitching. Many animals also evacuate their bladder or bowel. Do not be distressed – all this is purely reflex and does not mean that the dog is still alive. The pupils of the eye will dilate widely and the dog will not blink if the surface of the eye is touched. The heart will stop beating and respirations stop.

Deciding on a resting place

When a pet dies, you can feel grief, anger, guilt and confusion. Decision-making can be very difficult. You may have been tending to your dog intensively through an illness and then suddenly he is not there anymore. All that nurture and love suddenly has no subject and many people feel very lost and lonely. If the death was sudden, you may be totally unprepared and go into a form of shock.

When your dog is put to sleep in the veterinary surgery, the staff there will offer to dispose of the body. You may want to get out of surgery as quickly as possible and have a good cry on your own and accept their offer without considering the options. You may not have thought through what you want to do with the body. You may feel embarrassed asking what the options for the body are, but afterwards wish you had taken the body for burial or private cremation.

If you can face it, planning ahead is a sensible idea and the options outlined below may help you to decide what you would like to do. Some people feel that once their dog is dead its 'soul' or spirit has left, leaving merely an empty vessel. They are not concerned how the body is actually disposed of. Others wish to give the body a dignified and respectful farewell and this will be part of their grieving process. Other members of the family, especially the younger ones, may want to have a say in the matter. The procedure you decide on may also help you all come to terms with the death of your beloved pet.

Leaving the body with the vet

If you want to know what will actually happen to your dog's body if you leave it at the veterinary surgery, then ask. You do not need to wait until your dog has actually been put to sleep to find out. It may sound callous, but deceased pets which are put to sleep at veterinary surgeries, are officially defined as 'clinical waste' and have to be disposed of in an approved manner. Basically this means deep burial at a landfill site or incineration. Most surgeries arrange for pets to be cremated and this is generally thought to be the most acceptable method. Do not be frightened to ask your vet about what happens to pets that are put to sleep at that particular surgery and about any special arrangements, such as individual cremation or burial that can be made. They may have information about a local pet crematorium or cemetery .

To rest in the garden

Deciding that you want to bury your dog in your garden may depend on several factors – not the least being the size of the dog. If you are the owner of a giant breed you may need help to move the body and to dig a big enough hole. When Peter's nine-stone Bullmastiff was put to sleep the logistics of moving the body to the hole, which had taken all morning to dig, were quite complex and involved several people and a wheelbarrow!

Despite the efforts required, burial in the garden can be very reassuring. The close presence of the dog can be comforting and the grave can help to provide acceptance of loss. Home burial does require organisation, however this activity does enable you to tend to your animal for a little longer. That need to nurture and care is not cut off so abruptly, especially after a long period of close nursing. When your dog's need of you is suddenly gone, you may feel useless and a failure. Being able to do something usually helps.

You may wish to put the body in a casket or to have it cremated and bury the ashes (*see* Cremation, p. 116). Burying a favourite toy with your dog or wrapping it in its well-chewed blanket may also help you to put it into its final resting place. If you want to mark the spot with a headstone or plaque, there are many available from pet crematoria or masonry firms, Yellow Pages or popular animal magazines. Planting a rose, tree or shrub over the grave can be part of the ceremony and can provide a beautiful memorial. Seeing the plant grow and flourish somehow signals new life from old. There are hundreds of rose and other plant names that may be similar to that of your dog, its colour, favourite game or toy and can give special meaning to the plant over the grave.

The actual ceremony of burying the dog can help everyone, especially children, to accept that their pet is gone and will not come back. The grave offers a spot where they can go and talk to the animal if they want and at which they can direct their grief. It is a chance for the family to say goodbye and for children to see that is it acceptable for everyone to be upset. They can share in the grieving process rather than bottling up their feelings.

Pet cemeteries and crematoria

Many people want to cremate their dog or have a private service when it dies. There are now quite a few pet cemeteries and crematoria throughout the country, but it may be difficult to find one in your area or to know how good it is. Now many of the smaller specialised pet establishments have formed the Association of Private Pet Cemeteries and Crematoria. The members of the Association have published a code of conduct which they are all required to adhere to. Obviously all facilities are run independently and you must satisfy yourself on the range of services offered by each member and the fees they charge as these may vary greatly with area and the type of service provided. The members say they aim to give peace of mind by providing a dignified and caring farewell for pet companions.

You may choose a cemetery to bury your dog because it is a permanent site. Then house moves and the like do not matter, and the body has a permanent resting place. For some people the traditional graveyard setting is also what they want for their beloved dog. One of the criteria on the Association's code of conduct is that all members hold licences from their local authority so that the land is registered for use as a cemetery and the establishment cannot be closed down because of lack of planning permission.

You may want to visit the cemetery to see if you like the layout of the graves and the landscape, and to talk to the proprietors about the range of services available. The added benefit for those without transport is that the cemetery will often collect the dog's body from the vet's, prepare the grave and help with the burial. This includes supplying a casket if you want and offering a range of headstones for you to choose from.

There are some things to check out, however, if you do decide to use a pet cemetery:

- Look at the costs. Pet cemeteries do not come cheap.
- Find out if there is an annual maintainance fee to pay in addition to payment for looking after the grave.
- Check that the cemetery is built on consecrated ground. If not, there is always the risk, if the company goes out of business, that the land could be sold and used for something else.

- Check too, whether graves are permanent, or if they are cleared and re-used after a certain number of years.

Cremation

Just as many people opt for cremation, either because there is no space available for burial or simply because this is their wish, an increasing number of pets are cremated too. Cremation can be communal with several other pets, as often happens if the body is left at the veterinary surgery, or it can be a single event involving just your dog. Obviously, a single cremation will be more expensive, but some people are comforted to have their dog's ashes for burial themselves.

The crematorium may also collect the dog's body from the vet's so that this upsetting task is spared the owners. There are a number of companies around the country that perform this task. Make sure you ask them how they function and what facilities they have available. Ask, for example, if you can bring a dog's body for cremation; if you can be present at the cremation; if you will get a certificate guaranteeing that your dog was individually cremated and that the ashes you are given belong solely to your pet.

The Association of Private Pet Cemeteries and Crematorias has a code of conduct and membership list which can be send to you on receipt of an sae (address on page 121).

Obituaries and personal reminders

Do not be tempted to rush home from the veterinary surgery when your dog has been put to sleep and clear out all his or her toys or leads. They may cause you to feel sad because they remind you that he is not around, but you may well regret getting rid of everything and not keeping a memento of the dog, be it a toy, brush or lead. Lots of people keep bits and pieces their dog used or treasure photographs of their pet. It may sound silly and seem to be rather callous at the time, but if you do not have a picture of your dog and you know it is very ill, make the effort to take one or ask a friend to help. In time to come when the pain has mostly passed you may wish to talk about the dog and share experiences with others. Having a photograph to show and to remind you can be a great comfort. You may even wish to have a portrait painted from a photograph as a tribute to a really great canine friend – many artists advertise in dog magazines.

These magazines often have pages set aside for obituaries and this too can be a very comforting way of saying farewell to your dog as well as a public acknowledgement of your love for him and the gap which has been left in your life. Likewise a donation to an animal charity or to an area of veterinary research that is attempting to find a cure for the condition from which the dog died can feel like a worthwhile memorial. In this way future generations may be cured or survive longer thanks to your dog. No doubt by then you will be an owner again and be grateful for advances in veterinary medicine.

FEELINGS OF LOSS

When a pet dies, owners can feel sadness, grief, loneliness or severe depression. The loss can be very traumatic – to some, losing a dog can stir up memories of other losses, both human and animal, and the complex emotions can be very difficult to cope with. Because they feel that other people, especially those who have never owned a pet, may not understand the depth of their grief, some people will try to hide it. Many employers do not take kindly to a day missed at work because the dog or cat has died, especially if they have not had the same experience themselves. Most peole can cope on their own but many need a listening ear – expecially if the circumstances of loss are especially distressing, if the bond has been particularly strong or there is no one to understand among their friends and family.

The stages of grief

While everyone believes that what they feel is unique to them and that nobody else could understand how deeply upset they are, there are in fact common stages of mourning and grief. Although not everyone will experience all of these or even in the same order, most people will go through some aspects of this process. Stages can overlap and it may take a long time to get through the five recognised phases. Some people can become stuck at one stage or regress back to another during the grieving process.

SHOCK AND DISBELIEF Shock does not occur only if a death is sudden and unexpected; feelings of shock and disbelief can be brought on by the initial diagnosis of a terminal illness or the death which follows a long chronic condition. You may feel as if you are in a dream and that when you wake up everything will be fine. You are not really taking in what is happening – this can be much worse if the dog is lost without warning and you are still expecting it to wander in and ask to go for a walk. The news of a very poor prognosis from the vet can be met with disbelief and some people ask for a second opinion, no doubt holding out hope for a different diagnosis.

Most of us react to our pet's death by crying and small things, which may not even be associated with our dog, may send us over the fragile edge of self-control. Pyschologists tell us that it is good to cry and talk about the death rather than to bottle up our feelings. If you have the body of your dog at home you may want to wrap it in its favourite blanket, sit with it and stroke it for a while and gradually take in what has happened. It will give you a chance to say goodbye and have a last cuddle. You may even be reluctant to use the words dead, death or killed because you cannot yet accept that your dog has gone – time does not heal but it helps.

ANGER Anger is a common feeling after a death. The anger can be directed in many ways. You may 'blame' the veterinary surgeon whom you feel did not do enough – even though you know there was really nothing more that anyone could do. You may be angry at yourself for not noticing problems earlier, even though there may not have been any visible signs. You may even feel angry at the dog for dying and at other animals for being alive, even though you would not want anyone else to be going through what you are feeling. The feeling may not be logical, but it can still well up. Those around may need to be warned not to take any anger vented at them personally.

If you blame yourself because your dog had an accident when you feel you should have been watching it or had it under control, your guilt may be very intense. You may even fantasise about being able to turn back time and undo the situation, replaying the situation to change its outcome. You go over the incident again and again planning when you could have stopped the dog or remembering when you saw him for the last time and thinking . . . if only. You forget to think that, if you went through every moment of the day like this, you would be seeing an accident around every corner and would shut the dog in a padded room so nothing could ever happen.

One vet commented on the difficulty of timing the decision to have a pet put to sleep, saying that it was usually 'either 24 hours too early or 24 hours too late'. Either way owners feel guilty – the former because they feel they may have denied their dog some time and the latter that they may have let the dog suffer. It is doubtful that even trained and experienced vets get it 'right' with their own pets – they too are emotionally involved. You do your best for the dog and that is all he or she would expect from you.

BARGAINING If the vet has told you that there is nothing more he or she can do for your dog, you may try to bargain your way out of the situation with that higher authority. You may ask God to let the animal live in return for doing something you do not particularly like or that may cost you a lot of money. Some people proceed with costly treatment despite their awareness that it is unlikely to work.

DEEP SADNESS Sadness and depression can sit like a heavy weight on the chest. Sometimes when we are distracted and momentarily forget about the death of our dog, we are reminded of it again by this low heavy feeling. Just how long it lasts usually depends on the strength of the bond we had with that particular animal and often on how long we had it, although just because we have only owned an animal for a short period, it does not mean we are any the less affected by its death. It is said that this feeling of sadness starts a few hours after the pet dies and may reach a peak within two weeks. A dog which has been with you for perhaps 13 years is going to leave a huge gap in your life. Talking to someone who has gone through a similar experience can be a great help at this stage. Some non-pet owners may unknowingly say, 'It was just a dog – go out and get another one, after all it wasn't a person.' Not only have they underestimated the attachment a person can feel for a dog but they have made the grieving owner feel that it is socially unacceptable to be this upset about an animal rather than a person. Little do they know that the feelings are just the same, and sometimes more intense, at the loss of a pet.

ACCEPTANCE Passing throught the stages of shock, anger, guilt and sadness can take some time – there is no set limit. Time can help, as the adage goes, although it is hard to accept this immediately after the dog's death. After a while it is not quite so painful to look at photographs of the dog, to touch its toys or collar, or to speak its name. You may feel that you can start to look ahead and that you are ready to hear the patter of little paws around the house again, or at least to consider all the pros and cons of getting another dog. What is very important to realise is that the new one will never replace the old one and should never be compared – it is a personality in its own right and will bring its own set of joys and worries! It will, however, replace the old dog as an outlet for love, something to nurture and care for.

Help at hand

For some people the terrible feelings of loss and grief continue for a long time and they never embark on another relationship with an animal because they fear the same will happen when it goes. In one survey of veterinary clients who had lost a pet, 15 per cent said they would not wish to have another one because the emotional pain of loss was too great. Although most people manage to get through all the stages of grief and out the other side, some become stuck and do not reach the point where they can look back and smile at the good times. They cannot get over the loss of their dog and cannot reach the stage where they feel they can love another.

If you find that after a couple of months you still cannot cope with your grief there is a new service to help bereaved pet owners to overcome their feelings of sadness, grief, loneliness or depression which has recently been launched by the Society for Companion Animal Studies. The Society recognises the scale of the problems and offers a listening ear in the form of Befrienders. A network of these trained volunteers will provide the support that bereaved pet owners often need. All the Befrienders have experience of helping people overcome emotional difficulties. If you need to talk about a loss you can contact the SCAS Befriender helpline on 0891 615 285. You will be given the number of a local Befriender whom you can contact. One Befriender commented, 'When a pet dies it can have a devastating effect. Today people are not allowed to grieve and express their feelings if a special pet dies – emotions which are so natural and healthy to work through. People who have rung me feel isolated and lonely. One lady even asked me if she needed to go to a psychiatrist as people have made her feel such an emotional outcast over the loss of her pet.'

A wonderful little book entitled *Absent Friend* has been written by Laura and Martyn Lee. It is a compelling read as well as a great comfort if you have lost a pet. The book can be purchased for £5.95 (incl p. & p.) from Henston, The Chequers, 2 Church Street, High Wycombe, Bucks.

Appendix

Doggie wheelchairs – K-9 Carts, Mrs Barrow, Poplar Farm, Oxford Road, Oakley, Bucks HP18 9RQ

Bean bag beds and Dri Top cover – Barka Parka UK, 43 Bagworth Road, Nailstone, Nr Nuneaton, Warks CV13 0QJ

Electric pet bed heater – Petnap, 4 Hartham Lane, Biddlestone, Chippenham, Wilts SN14 7EA

Raised feeding and water bowls – Luxway Canine Supplies, Brabourne Lees, Ashford, Kent TN25 5LG

Waterproof pads – Over The Top Textiles, Bernard Stuart Ltd, Barley Hill House, Chadlington, Oxon OX7 3NU

Flectabed bedding – Serendipity, PO Box 226, Castle Donington, Derby DE7 2YN

Help carrying dog – Helping Hand from Mikki Products, Hamelin House, 211 - 213 High Town Road, Luton, Beds LU2 0BZ

Flexilead – Flexi (UK) Ltd, Unit 4 Chapel Road, Portslade, Brighton, Sussex

Car harness – sizes for dogs from Yorkie to Rottweiler size from Luxway Canine Supplies (see above)

Homesitters, Buckland Wharf, Buckland, Aylesbury HP22 5LQ

Staywell Pet Doors – Blackpool Road, Preston, Lancs PR2 2DN

Association of Pet Cemeteries and Crematoria, 22 Westerleigh Road, Pucklechurch, Bristol BS17 3PY

John Fisher's Dog Training Discs, Greengarth, Maddox Lane, Bookham, Surrey KT23 3HT

Vetbed is available from Petlife, Minster House, Weston Way, Bury St Edmunds, Suffolk IP33 3SU

ACKNOWLEDGEMENTS

Our grateful thanks are due to the readers of *Dogs Today* and the *Bristol Evening Post* who completed the Golden Oldies survey and who gave us the inspiration for this book. Their time and effort in filling in the questionnaire and their obvious love of their oldies gave us a great deal of information, which we hope will be of value to all owners of older dogs. To Clare T, too, for her help with the survey and patience on the computer!